"What a wonderful workbook! Even for those of us who feel w
self-esteem, this book provides insight and techniques for impro
sometimes make us question ourselves and our self-worth. Wi
difficult physical therapy patients, I often employ the cognitive r
acknowledging what is 'right' about themselves to break the
themselves or their situation. This in itself often leads to an acceleration in the healing process."



—Linda C. Harvey, M.A., P.T., Physical Therapy Role Extender for Rehabilitation Coordinator, Visiting Nurses Association of Maryland

"Every page is full of profound ideas to clarify the value of positive self-esteem. The easy exercises promote deep contemplation of how we paint a picture of our current selves and then give solid directions on improving that perception. It is impossible to read this book without feeling better about oneself and others. It should be required reading for every living soul."

—Robert L. Bunnell, M.S., PA-C, marketing coordinator, University of Utah Physician Assistant Program Executive Director, Utah Academy of Physician Assistants

"The book is excellent. We are already using it in our self-esteem presentations! Well done and many thanks . . . It's one of the first and finest self-esteem resource guide books that offers in-depth information in a grounded, useful way."

—Jacqueline Miller, Maryland Governor's Task Force on Self-Esteem

"As a former legislative aide to John Vasconcellos and the Self-Esteem effort, I found the book to be practical and impactful in its suggested activities. It can enlighten the thinking and enrich a person's experience of their own self-esteem."

—Andy Michael, Aide to Assemblyman John Vasconcellos, California Task Force on Self-Esteem

"I was first introduced to these mental health principles and skills as a student in Schiraldi's *Stress and the Healthy Mind* course. Not only have they proven useful for helping certain friends and family members, but I have also taken every opportunity to teach them to my students and the student teachers I supervise. Of the many self-esteem books on the market, this is the only one I know that actually equips readers with the skills necessary to effect changes in their own lives."

—Stephen L. Brown, Ph.D., Southern Illinois University

"Glenn Schiraldi has created a hands-on program that can be used as a complete program or for counselors wishing to add specific exercises to treatment. This book is certainly appropriate for continuing education of counselors as well as an office manual. The material is current and well organized."

—Thomas W. Clawson, Executive Director, National Board of Certified Counselors

"Glenn Schiraldi challenges our previous understanding of self-esteem as a somewhat esoteric concept through a unique and refreshing approach that is brilliant in its simplicity. The approach unfolds logically, beginning with a definition and supporting model, followed by a holistic, realistic skill-building approach to nurturing self-esteem . . . simply brilliant. As evidence of the book's versatility and richness and the best endorsement that I could give a book, I have used it extensively as a mental health resource, as an invaluable teaching tool for courses with college students, and as a gift to close friends."

—Melissa Hallmark Kerr, M.A., Ph.D., college instructor, health consultant

"I began reading *The Self-Esteem Workbook* largely to help others, and I was surprised to find it was a great help to me too. We all need a boost in our self-esteem. I have given the book to others."

—Tracey A. Shoopack, M.B.A., contracts manager

"Glenn Schiraldi's methods are grounded in research and real-life application. Being able to work directly with him changed the way that I view stress management. In lieu of working with Glenn daily, being able to read, and reread, his book has enhanced my life in countless ways."

—S. Kathleen Jennings, former student of Glenn Schiraldi

"It's obvious that this book is a labor of love that was many years in the making. It shows that self-esteem can be increased, regardless of one's upbringing, past environment, and experiences. The readings and exercises provide concrete steps to establish unconditional self-worth and cultivate the skill of love. I particularly enjoyed the inspirational quotes from men and women who have realized their self-worth and thus been able to reach out beyond themselves. This book is a great personal investment!"

—Pamela G. Barainca, R.D., L.D., clinical dietitian

"Even successful people have self-defeating ideas that impair self-esteem. At least one idea from every page has affected myself, my life, and every single person that I have spoken to in my professional life."

—Mohammad Beiraghdar, medical student

"I found *The Self-Esteem Workbook* to be an infinitely deep wellspring in my work as a volunteer facilitator for groups of victims of abuse. It is clear and easy to understand and its step-by-step program is perfect for those struggling with self-worth issues. Its timeless content applies to anyone suffering with low self-esteem. I have used it over and over and will continue to do so. Thank you Glenn Schiraldi!"

—Janet Harkness, homemaker, mother

# The Self-Esteem Workbook

Glenn R. Schiraldi, Ph.D.

New Harbinger Publications, Inc.

*Publisher's Note*



The authors and/or publisher have generously given permission to reprint and/or use extended quotations or entire works from the following copyrighted material: From *Lifesigns: Intimacy, Fecundity and Ecstasy* by H. J. Nouwen. Copyright 1986. Reprinted by permission of Doubleday. The poem *If I Could Be* by Ken Kirk. Reprinted by permission of Ken Kirk. From *Hope and Help for Depression: A Practical Guide* by Glenn Schiraldi. Copyright 1990. Reprinted by permission of Glenn Schiraldi. From *It's You I Like* by Fred Rodgers. Copyright 1970. Used by permission of Fred M. Rogers and Family Communications, Inc., Pittsburgh, PA. "Body Appreciation," slightly condensed from *Wisdom, Purpose, and Love* by Jack Canfield. Copyright 1985. Reprinted by permission of Jack Canfield, coauthor *Chicken Soup for the Soul* series. "The Pleasant Events Schedule" and instructions adapted from *Control Your Depression* by P. M. Lewinsohn, R. F. Munoz, M. A. Youngren, and A. M. Zeiss. Copyright 1986. By permission of Peter M. Lewinsohn. From "The Little Things That Make Life Worth Living" in the *Providence Journal-Bulletin*. Reprinted by permission of Mark Patinkin. Corrective experiences from *Healing the Shame That Binds You* by John Bradshaw and *Cycles of Power* by P. Levin. Reprinted with permission of Health Communications, Inc. *Love Finds a Way* by Bob Greene. Reprinted by permission of Tribune Media Services, Inc. All Rights Reserved. *Rational Responses to Four of Ellis' Irrational Beliefs* by Russell A. Bourne, Jr., Ph.D., chief of staff, the Upledger Institute, Palm Beach Gardens, FL Reprinted by permission of Russell A. Bourne, Jr. Preassessment questions, laws of human worth, original list of externals, diagrams of worth as separate from externals and contrasting ways to conceptualize human worth, example of failure to be promoted, and the "Nevertheless Skills" from Claudia A. Howard, Individual Potential Seminars, 606 S. Davis Street, West, TX.

Distributed in the U.S.A. by Publishers Group West; in Canada by Raincoast Books; in Great Britain by Airlift Book Company, Ltd.; in South Africa by Real Books, Ltd.; in Australia by Boobook; and in New Zealand by Tandem Press.


New Harbinger Publications, Inc.
5674 Shattuck Avenue
Oakland, CA 94609

Originally published as *Building Self-Esteem* in 1993 by Kendall/Hunt Publishing Company and in 1999 by Chevron Publishing Company.

Cover design by Poulson/Gluck Design
Edited by Jueli Gastwirth

Library of Congress number: 01-132281
ISBN 1-57224-252-3 Paperback



Printed in the United States of America

New Harbinger Publications' Web site address: www.newharbinger.com

03 02 01

10 9 8 7 6 5 4 3

When we plant a rose seed in the earth, we notice that it is small, but we do not criticize it as "rootless and stemless." We treat it as a seed, giving it the water and nourishment required of a seed. When it first shoots up out of the earth, we don't condemn it as immature and underdeveloped, nor do we criticize the buds for not being open when they appear. We stand in wonder at the process taking place and give the plant the care it needs at each stage of its development. The rose is a rose from the time it is a seed to the time it dies. Within it, at all times, it contains its whole potential. It seems to be constantly in the process of change; yet at each state, at each moment, it is [whole] as it is (Gallwey 1974).

*I dedicate this work to my angel mother, who—like so many mothers throughout history—has quietly modeled so many of the principles described herein.*

# Contents


| | | |
|---|---|---|
| | Acknowledgments | ix |
| | Introduction | 1 |

PART I
UNDERSTANDING SELF-ESTEEM

| | | |
|---|---|---|
| **Chapter 1** | Why Self-Esteem? | **5** |
| **Chapter 2** | Getting Ready: The Physical Preparation | **9** |
| **Chapter 3** | Self-Esteem and How It Develops | **19** |

PART II
FACTOR I
THE REALITY OF UNCONDITIONAL HUMAN WORTH

| | | |
|---|---|---|
| **Chapter 4** | The Basics of Human Worth | **29** |

| | | |
|---|---|---|
| **Chapter 5** | Recognize and Replace Self-Defeating Thoughts | **39** |
| **Chapter 6** | Acknowledge Reality: "Nevertheless!" | **53** |
| **Chapter 7** | Regard Your Core Worth | **57** |
| **Chapter 8** | Create the Habit of Core-Affirming Thoughts | **63** |
| **Chapter 9** | An Overview of Unconditional Human Worth | **67** |

FACTOR II
EXPERIENCING UNCONDITIONAL LOVE

| | | |
|---|---|---|
| **Chapter 10** | The Basics of Unconditional Love | **71** |
| **Chapter 11** | Find, Love, and Heal the Core Self | **77** |
| **Chapter 12** | The Language of Love | **83** |
| **Chapter 13** | The Good Opinion of Others | **89** |
| **Chapter 14** | Acknowledge and Accept Positive Qualities | **93** |
| **Chapter 15** | Cultivate Body Appreciation | **99** |
| **Chapter 16** | Reinforce and Strengthen Body Appreciation | **105** |
| **Chapter 17** | Assert Self-Love and Appreciation | **109** |
| **Chapter 18** | Eyes of Love Meditation | **113** |
| **Chapter 19** | Liking the Face in the Mirror | **115** |
| **Chapter 20** | An Overview of Unconditional Love | **117** |

FACTOR III
THE ACTIVE SIDE OF LOVE: GROWING

| | | |
|---|---|---|
| **Chapter 21** | The Basics of Growing | **121** |
| **Chapter 22** | Accept That You Aren't Perfect | **129** |
| **Chapter 23** | Just for the Fun of It (Contemplating Possibilities) | **133** |
| **Chapter 24** | Take Stock of Your Character | **137** |
| **Chapter 25** | Experience Pleasure | **143** |
| **Chapter 26** | Prepare for Setbacks | **151** |
| **Chapter 27** | An Overview of Growing | **161** |
| **Epilogue** | Summing Up | **165** |

## Appendices

**Appendix I** Model for Helping the Person in Distress **169**

**Appendix II** Forgiving the Self **173**

**Appendix III** Touching the Past with Love **175**

Recommended Readings **179**

Bibliography **181**

# Acknowledgments

No one sees clearly without standing on the shoulders of those who have preceded us.

I'd like to first thank the late Morris Rosenberg, professor of sociology, University of Maryland. Dr. Rosenberg's theorizing, meticulous research, and teaching have stimulated my own thinking on self-esteem immeasurably. Similarly, I am grateful to the late Dr. Stanley Coopersmith, whose germinal research combined with Dr. Rosenberg's provide the theoretical foundations of this book.

Special thanks go to Claudia Howard, whose patient dialogue, theoretical insights, and practical ideas lifted my thinking far beyond where it would have gone otherwise.

Thanks to Dr. John Burt, dean of the College of Health and Human Performance, who taught me to make thinking a hobby. Teaming with him in teaching his "Ways of Knowing about Human Stress and Tension" allowed me to first wrestle with turning theory regarding stress and self-esteem into practice.

And thanks to the students of the University of Maryland, some older, some younger, who have helped me to sharpen the theory and practice of teaching self-esteem.

I express gratitude to the cognitive theorists and practitioners who influenced chapter 5. Albert Ellis originated the ABC model, catastrophizing, and shoulds. Aaron Beck originated Automatic Thoughts, the term "distortions," most of the distortions presently used in cognitive therapy, the idea of basic (core) beliefs, and the idea of recording thoughts, distortions, and moods. David Burns wrote *Feeling Good*, a very useful application of Beck's theories. With great gratitude, I also acknowledge those who inspired chapter 15, including Russell M. Nelson (*The*

*Power Within Us*), L. Schlossberg and G. D. Zuidema (*The Johns Hopkins Atlas of Human Functional Anatomy*), National Geographic Society (*The Incredible Machine*), and J. D. Ratcliff (*I Am Joe's ...* series).

I am particularly appreciative of Bev Monis, who produced this manuscript with saintly patience, and Carol Jackson, who created the beautiful graphics for the original edition, and upon which this edition's graphics were based.

Finally, I wish to acknowledge with sincere gratitude all the wonderful, conscientious, and encouraging people at New Harbinger Publications, especially Patrick Fanning, Jueli Gastwirth, Kasey Pfaff, Amy Shoup, and Michele Waters.

# Introduction

*We need to see ourselves as basic miracles.*

—Virginia Satir

Self-esteem is not the only determinant of happiness. Certainly it is one of the most important.

The beloved late comedian George Burns (1984) observed that most of the things that make people happy—health, marriage, raising a family, self-respect, etc.—do not fall into our laps. We "have to work at them a little."

And so it is with self-esteem. Like cultivating a garden, building self-esteem involves consistent effort. The program described in this book takes approximately a half hour a day, more or less, over a 125-day period. Is this investment worth it? When we consider how great the effect of self-esteem is on mental and physical well-being, in both the short and long term, few efforts seem more worthwhile.

The program you are about to start is the central component of "Stress and the Healthy Mind," a course that I developed and taught at the University of Maryland. The course has been found to raise self-esteem while reducing symptoms of depression, anxiety, and hostility among adults eighteen to sixty-eight years of age (Schiraldi and Brown 2001; Brown and Schiraldi 2000). Although intended for adults, the principles and skills in this book are equally applicable to adolescents and, when slightly simplified, children.

# Part I

# Understanding Self-Esteem

# Chapter 1

# Why Self-Esteem?

How fortunate is the person with self-esteem. There is general agreement that self-esteem is central to good mental and physical health, while self-dislike degrades health and performance. Self-dislike appears to contribute to:

- Depression
- Anxiety
- Stress symptoms
- Psychosomatic illness, like headaches, insomnia, fatigue, and digestive tract upset
- Hostility, excessive or deep-seated anger, dislike and distrust of others, competitiveness
- Spouse and child abuse
- Entering into abusive/unhappy relationships
- Alcohol and drug abuse
- Eating disorders and unhealthy dieting
- Poor communication (e.g., non-assertive, aggressive, defensive, critical, or sarcastic styles)
- Promiscuity

- Dependency
- Sensitivity to criticism
- Tendency to put on a false front to impress others
- Social difficulties—withdrawal, loneliness
- Poor performance/classroom achievement
- Preoccupation with problems
- Status concern

No wonder self-dislike is called the invisible handicap. Conversely, self-esteem is highly correlated to overall life satisfaction. In a 1992 Gallup survey, 89 percent of respondents said that self-esteem is very important in motivating a person to work hard and succeed. Self-esteem was ranked higher as a motivator than any other variable. It is not surprising, therefore, that those with self-esteem are more likely to engage in healthy behaviors. Those with self-esteem tend to be friendlier, more expressive, more active, more self-trusting and trusting of others, and less troubled by inner problems and criticism (Coopersmith 1967). When mental disorders do strike, those with self-esteem tend to respond better to professional help, while recovering alcoholics with self-esteem are less likely to relapse (Mecca, Smelser, and Vasconcellos 1989). (See Appendix I: Model for Helping the Person in Distress). Indeed, one searches the literature in vain to find a disadvantage of having self-esteem. Thus, an assumption of this book is that self-esteem not only helps reduce undesired stress and illness symptoms, but also is an essential foundation for human growth.

Despite the importance of self-esteem, surprisingly little attention has been focused on building it directly rather than indirectly. For example, an oft-stated aim of psychotherapy is to build self-esteem. However, the assumption that reducing illness symptoms will indirectly build self-esteem is unsupported. Lacking a comprehensive approach, some well-intending individuals have prescribed quick fixes based on unsound principles, which can actually damage self-esteem in the long run.

This book provides a step-by-step plan based on sound principles to help you build a healthy, realistic, and generally stable self-esteem. The approach requires that the skills herein be applied and practiced. Merely having knowledge is not enough. Each self-esteem skill is based on mastery of the skills that precede it. As Abraham Maslow noted, developing self-esteem requires many and major impacts (Lowry 1973). Therefore, resist the tendency to read through this book quickly. Instead, commit now to applying and mastering each skill before moving on to try the next one.

## To Begin

The following Self-Esteem Checkup will provide you with a starting point from which to measure your progress as you read through this book. Taking the checkup will also begin to reinforce some of the goals of this book. It is comforting to realize that each person already possesses some measure of self-esteem to build on. There is nothing tricky about this checkup, nor is it important how your scores compare with the scores of others. So just relax and be as completely honest as you can.

## The Self-Esteem Checkup

First, rate from 0 to 10 how much you believe each of the following statements. 0 means you completely disbelieve it. 10 means you think it is completely true.

| **Statement** | **Rating** |
|---|---|
| 1. I am a worthwhile person. | ______ |
| 2. I am as valuable as a person as anyone else. | ______ |
| 3. I have the qualities I need to live well. | ______ |
| 4. When I look into my eyes in the mirror I have a pleasant feeling. | ______ |
| 5. I don't feel like an overall failure. | ______ |
| 6. I can laugh at myself. | ______ |
| 7. I am happy to be me. | ______ |
| 8. I like myself, even when others reject me. | ______ |
| 9. I love and support myself, regardless of what happens. | ______ |
| 10. I am generally satisfied with the way I am developing as a person. | ______ |
| 11. I respect myself. | ______ |
| 12. I'd rather be me than someone else. | ______ |
| **Total Score** | ______ |

Next, rate your self-esteem on the following scales (Gauthier, Pellerin, and Renaud 1983):

| 0 | 100 |
|---|---|
| Total lack of self-esteem | Total fullness of self-esteem |

**Your Response** ______

How often do you feel restricted in your daily activities because of difficulties with self-esteem?

| 1 | 2 | 3 | 4 | 5 |
|---|---|---|---|---|
| Always | Often | Sometimes | Rarely | Never |

**Your Response** ______

How serious is your problem with self-esteem?

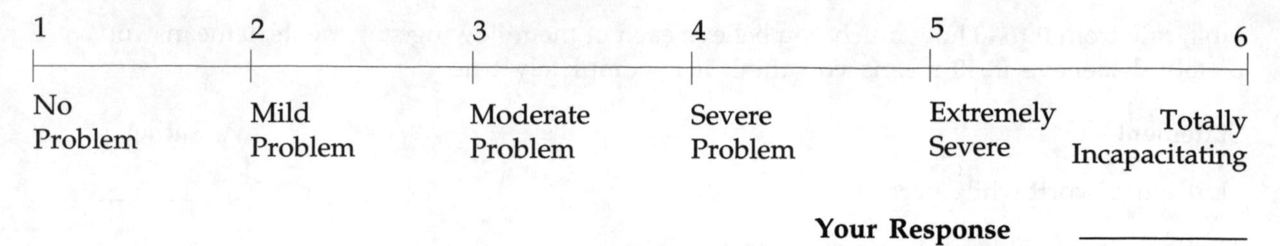


**Your Response** ___________

# Chapter 2

# Getting Ready: The Physical Preparation

The mind and body are connected. If you want to feel your best mentally, take good care of your body. This only stands to reason. So often people who feel stressed, fatigued, and mentally "down" are under-exercised, undernourished, and under-rested. Often, they assume that tending the body takes too much time or is too difficult. So they hope for a quick fix that allows them to ignore their basic physical needs, while their mental health and performance suffer. The point is important enough to restate: You can't ignore your body and expect to feel good. Time invested in physical health is a wise investment indeed. It saves time by sharpening your performance. More importantly, it improves mental health.

The object of this chapter is to help you set up and execute a simple, written plan for optimal physical health in three areas: aerobic exercise, sleep hygiene, and eating practices.

## Aerobic Exercise

Exercise improves self-esteem (Sonstroem 1984) and general mental health (Morgan 1984). Exercise is also the treatment of choice for weight control and sleep improvement. The goal here is at least twenty minutes of aerobic exercise most days. Strength and flexibility training are very useful, and confer additional benefits. If time permits, you can add these to your program. If not, or if adding these appears overwhelming, then be content with aerobic exercise. Aerobic exercise is continuous, rhythmic exercise that keeps the heart rate gently elevated. Aerobic exercise includes walking, biking, rowing, swimming, and jogging. The best exercise choice is probably the one you enjoy doing most. Moderate, regular exercise is the goal.

Walking daily for thirty minutes can be quite effective for losing weight and for stress management. Adding strength training also helps lose fat because muscles burn energy rapidly. However, don't be overwhelmed. Any amount of exercise is better than none. Even a ten-minute "energy walk," an exercise break from sitting at the desk, has been found to increase energy and lift the mood (Thayer 1989).

Start your exercise gently, and build up gradually. You are not in a competition with anyone. Exercise should leave you feeling refreshed and energized. It should not hurt or exhaust you beyond a pleasant fatigue. If you can eventually work up to twenty minutes or more on most days, great. If not, do what you can to start. Do make a plan for regular, moderate exercise. If you have trouble falling asleep, try exercising before dinner, or earlier. Consult your physician if you are over forty years old, if you have any known risk factors for cardiovascular disease, and/or if you have any concerns about starting an exercise program.

## Sleep Hygiene

Poor sleep has been associated with unhappiness in many studies (Diener 1984). Much has been learned in recent years about sleep hygiene and the treatment of sleep disorders. Two considerations are crucial: the amount and regularity.

### *An Appropriate Amount of Sleep*

Most adults require at least eight hours of sleep. Preliminary research indicates that adults who average near that amount, but then get an additional hour or hour and a half, feel better and perform better. However, today's lifestyle nibbles away at sleep, so that many adults are chronically sleep deprived.

### *Regularity of Sleep*

Regular sleep and wake-up times are needed to keep the body's sleep cycle consistent. Retiring at irregular hours (e.g., getting to bed much later on Friday and Saturday nights than on the weekdays) can lead to exhaustion and even sleep disorders.

So the idea is to get a little more sleep than you think you need, and to keep sleep and wake-up times as consistent throughout the week as possible, varying no more than one hour from night to night.

## Eating Practices

If you visualize a plate where meat is the small side serving, and plant foods fill the rest of the plate, then you have a pretty good idea of eating goals, which include:

- Consume most of your calories from complex carbohydrates, which come from plant foods (fruits, vegetables, breads, rice, pasta, cereals, etc.). Foods that are fresh, frozen, or minimally processed are better choices than processed fóod because they tend to have more fiber and less added sugar, salt, and fat.

- Reduce consumption of meat, which contains saturated fats and cholesterol, to about six ounces daily. Use mainly lean meats, poultry without skin, fish, or meat alternatives, like dry beans and peas, or nuts.
- Reduce fats, sugar, salt, caffeine, processed foods, and alcohol. If sleep is troubled, avoid caffeine altogether for at least seven hours before bedtime.
- Ingest adequate calcium. Adults nineteen to fifty years of age need at least 1,000 mg of calcium. A glass of skim milk provides 300 mg. If you drink three glasses of skim milk (or eat yogurt or cheese equivalents), then additional calcium is still needed from sources like spinach, broccoli, fortified orange juice, or tofu.

Additional guidelines that can generally improve health, help control weight, and help elevate the mood include:

- Keep blood sugar steady throughout the day. This can be done by eating breakfast, not skipping meals, and eating smaller, more frequent meals. There is evidence that eating five to six smaller meals reduces fatigue and mood swings, while facilitating weight loss. "Meals" can include healthy midmorning and midafternoon snacks of a half sandwich, yogurt, a fruit, etc. Avoid concentrated sweets, which cause blood sugar fluctuations.
- Shift food, so that some of the calories that would normally be eaten at a big dinner are eaten at breakfast, lunch, or snacks.
- Choose foods often that are less than 30 percent fat. To quickly estimate, multiply the grams of fat by ten and divide by the total calories. The result should be less that 33 percent. For example, a candy bar contains 250 calories and 14 grams of fat. Thus:

  $$\frac{14 \text{ grams fat} \times 10}{250 \text{ calories}} = 56 \text{ percent}$$

  This example is quite high in fat. The sugar would also tend to give a momentary energy lift, but would make people more tired and tense an hour later (a brisk walk would give a similar energy lift that would be sustained). Similar calculations for bread, potatoes, or almost all other plant products (before adding butter or oil) would show these to be healthy choices. Although meat can exceed the 30 percent fat goal, meats can be mixed with vegetables to reduce overall fat (e.g., meat stir-fried in a little oil).

## Take Care of Your Body: A Written Plan

There is power in making a written plan and committing to stick to it. Please make a plan that you can follow, and begin to practice it for the next fourteen days. You'll actually stay with this plan throughout the entire course of this book and beyond, so make a realistic plan that you can comfortably keep. It is perfectly all right to give yourself several days to "work up" to the goals in your plan.

1. **Exercise**. At least four to five times per week; at least twenty minutes of aerobic exercise. Describe your plan below:

2. **Sleep**. ________ hours/night (a little more than you think you need) from _______________ (time you'll retire) to _______________ (time you'll wake up).

3. **Eating**. At least three times a day, using healthy choices. Make a written week's menu using the worksheet on the next page and check it against the eating goals and dietary guidelines that follow.

## Sample Menu: A Week of Meals

Write down what you plan to eat and drink each day, and the amounts of food/liquid.

| | Mon | Tue | Wed | Thu | Fri | Sat | Sun |
|---|---|---|---|---|---|---|---|
| Breakfast | | | | | | | |
| Snack | | | | | | | |
| Lunch | | | | | | | |
| Snack | | | | | | | |
| Dinner | | | | | | | |
| Snack | | | | | | | |

## Dietary Guidelines

Check to see if your sample menu meets the following guidelines for healthy eating:

1. Does your plan provide the daily recommended servings from each food group as indicated below? (Someone trying to control weight would use the smaller figure for servings.)

| Food Group | Servings needed per day | Examples of one serving |
|---|---|---|
| Breads, cereals, rice, pasta | 6–11 | 1 slice bread<br>1 oz ready-to-eat cereal<br>½ bun or bagel<br>½ C cooked cereal, rice, or pasta |
| Vegetables | 3–5 | 1 C raw leafy greens<br>½ C other kinds of vegetables<br>¾ C vegetable juice |
| Fruits | 2–4 | 1 medium apple, banana, or orange<br>½ C fresh, chopped, cooked, or canned fruit<br>¾ C fruit juice |
| Milk, yogurt, and cheese | 2–3 | 1 C milk or yogurt (skim or low fat is best)<br>1½ oz natural cheese<br>2 oz processed cheese |
| Meats, poultry, fish, dry beans and peas, eggs, and nuts | 2–3 | Amounts to a total of approx. 6 oz a day, where 1 serving is 2-3 oz of cooked lean meat, poultry, or fish. Count as 1 oz meat: 1 egg; 2 tbs peanut butter; ½ C cooked, dry beans or peas; ⅓ C nuts; or ¼ C seeds |

2. Does your plan provide variety? That is, do you vary your choices within each group? (e.g., Instead of an apple each day, try bananas or strawberries as alternatives.)
3. Does your plan follow the other guidelines previously stated under Eating Practices?

## An Initial Fourteen Day Commitment

Keep a daily record for fourteen days to see how well you stick to your plan. Throughout the fourteen days make whatever adjustments you need, and then continue the plan as you read the rest of the book. Sometime during these initial fourteen days, complete the Preassessment and Assessing Your Reaction sections that follow. Proceed to chapter 3 only after you have completed these three steps.

### *A Daily Record*

| Day | Date | Exercised (minutes) | Number of meals eaten | Sleep | | |
|---|---|---|---|---|---|---|
| | | | | Hours | Time to bed | Time out of bed |
| 1 | | | | | | |
| 2 | | | | | | |
| 3 | | | | | | |
| 4 | | | | | | |
| 5 | | | | | | |
| 6 | | | | | | |
| 7 | | | | | | |
| 8 | | | | | | |
| 9 | | | | | | |
| 10 | | | | | | |
| 11 | | | | | | |
| 12 | | | | | | |
| 13 | | | | | | |
| 14 | | | | | | |

## *Preassessment*

Sit comfortably. Take a few deep breaths, relax and answer the following questions in writing.

1. Where is your self-esteem lately? Some answer this question simply, as in low, medium or high, or on a scale from one to ten. For some, responses are more complex. You might note, for instance, that your self-esteem, in truth, fluctuates, or that, although you are growing stronger, you still struggle with mistakes you make or have made, or with expectations you or others have. There is power and courage in honestly acknowledging what is. Just observe where you are now, without judging yourself, or wondering what others might think.

2. How did your family of origin contribute to your self-esteem, for good and bad?

3. What have you learned to do to increase your self-esteem?

4. What, if anything, can make you inferior as a person?

5. What, if anything, can make you superior as a person?

6. Using an artistic medium—colored pens or pencils, paint, crayons, finger paints, etc.—draw your opinion of yourself on a separate sheet of paper. There is something revealing and almost magical in expressing without words how you experience yourself.

The answers to questions three, four, and five especially can provide insight into what can ultimately strengthen self-esteem, although not in the ways most people think. Did you notice that the very things that raise self-esteem can also threaten it? For example, if getting a raise at work lifts your self-esteem, does failing to get a promotion cause it to fall? If a compliment makes you *feel* superior, does criticism make you feel inferior? If love raises self-esteem, does a relationship that does not work well destroy it?

Many assume that we get value from what we do, from skills, talents, and character traits, or from acceptance from others. While all of these are desirable, I suggest that none of these make good first steps for self-esteem building. Where, then, does human value come from?

## Assessing Your Reaction

"I do not want to suggest that productivity is wrong or needs to be despised. On the contrary, productivity and success can greatly enhance our lives. But when our value as human beings depends on what we make with our hands and minds, we become victims of the fear tactics of our world. When productivity is our main way of overcoming self-doubt, we are extremely vulnerable to rejection and criticism and prone to inner anxiety and depression. Productivity can never give the deep sense of belonging we crave. The more we produce, the more we realize that successes and results cannot give us the experience of 'at homeness.' In fact, our productivity often reveals to us that we are driven by fear. In this sense, sterility and productivity are the same: both can be signs that we doubt our ability to live fruitful lives" (Nouwen 1986).

What does this quote mean to you? Answer in four complete sentences.

1. ______________________________

______________________________

______________________________

______________________________

2. ______________________________

______________________________

______________________________

______________________________

3. ______________________________

______________________________

______________________________

______________________________

4. ______________________________

______________________________

______________________________

______________________________

If, as Nouwen suggests, worth and perhaps mental well-being are not consequences of productivity, what in your view *does* promote a sense of worth and well-being? Are these teachable? How would you teach them to a child?

Nouwen continues:

> "Living with Jean Vanier and his handicapped people, I realize how success-oriented I am. Living with men and women who cannot compete in the worlds of business, industry, sports, or academics, but for whom dressing, walking, speaking, eating, drinking, and playing are the main 'accomplishments,' is extremely frustrating for me. I may have come to the theoretical insight that being is more important than doing, but when asked to just be with people who can do very little I realize how far I am from the realization of that insight. Thus, the handicapped have become my teachers, telling me in many different ways that productivity is something other than fecundity. Some of us might be productive and others not, but we are all called to bear fruit; fruitfulness is a true quality of love."

Do you think that there are handicaps worse than physical ones?

If you were handicapped (mentally, physically, or emotionally), what kind of mindsets might keep you from insanity?

## Chapter 3

# Self-Esteem and How It Develops

What leads to self-esteem? The research is very clear. If you want to have self-esteem, it helps to choose your parents well. Children with self-esteem tend to have parents who model self-esteem. These parents consistently are loving toward their children, expressing interest in the child's life and friends, giving time and encouragement. I am reminded of the man who said to his neighbor, "Why did you spend all day with your son fixing that bike, when the bike shop could have fixed it in an hour?" The neighbor replied, "Because I am building a son, not fixing a bike."

Parents of children with self-esteem have high standards and expectations, but the expectations are clear, reasonable, consistent, and given with support and encouragement. The disciplinary style is democratic, which is to say that the child's opinions and individuality are respected, but the parents make the final decisions on matters of importance.

In short, the parents give messages that say, in effect, "I trust you, but I also recognize that you are not perfect. Still, I love you, and therefore will take time to guide you, set limits, discipline you, and expect the best of you because I believe in you and value you." These messages are far different from the distrust conveyed by the authoritarian parent, or the lack of caring conveyed by the permissive parent.

Some individuals have none of these parental antecedents, yet still have self-esteem. So this leads to a most important question: In the absence of these antecedents, how does one build self-esteem? Most assume we get value from what we do, from skills, character traits, talents, or acceptance of others. Again, I suggest that none of these make a good starting place for self-esteem building. Where, then, do we start? Let's begin by examining what self-esteem is.

## What Is Self-Esteem?

In principle, self-esteem is generally stable, but it can fluctuate, even from day to day, according to thought patterns, which can be influenced by, among other things: physical health, chemistry, appearance, and relationships. The fact that self-esteem can fluctuate is reason for optimism, because it suggests that self-esteem can change.

The definition of self-esteem is central to our journey. *Self-esteem* is a realistic, appreciative opinion of oneself. *Realistic* means accurate and honest. *Appreciative* implies positive feelings and liking. Some speak of high and low self-esteem, but this makes self-esteem seem like a numbers game that is competitive and comparative. It's preferable to say simply that people possess self-esteem when they have a realistic and appreciative opinion of themselves. The figure below clarifies the meaning of self-esteem. Self-esteem is squarely between *self-defeating shame* and *self-defeating pride.*

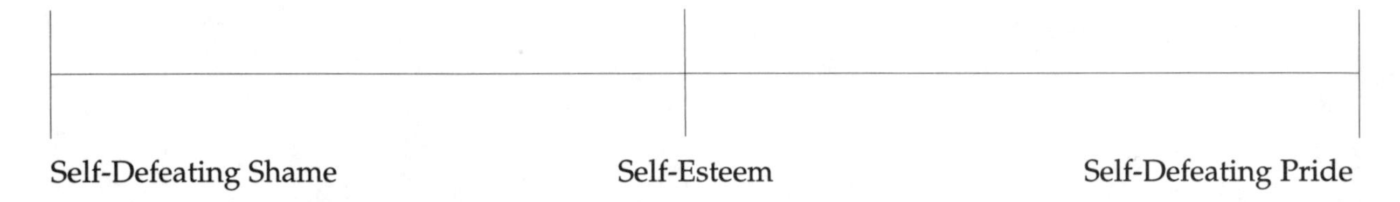

Self-Defeating Shame Self-Esteem Self-Defeating Pride

People with *self-defeating pride* are trying to be more than human. They are arrogant, and narcissistic, which means that they think they are better and more important than others as a person. Their view of others is vertical, or comparative, which is to say that to be on top means others must be below them. Self-defeating pride is often rooted in insecurity. Explore the lives of famous dictators, and you often find a complete lack of the parental antecedents that were discussed earlier.

People with *self-defeating shame*, or *self-defeating humility*, believe that they are less than human. They view people vertically, and see themselves as the dust of the earth. They hold an unrealistic and unappreciative opinion of themselves.

By contrast to the above views, people with *self-esteem* believe they are neither more or less than human. Knowing their faults and rough edges, they still are deeply and quietly glad to be who they are (Briggs 1977). They are like the good friend who knows you well and likes you anyway because they recognize the goodness, excellence, and potential that coexist alongside imperfections. People with self-esteem view others as equals, on a level or horizontal plane.

## Concepts Related to Self-Esteem

Self-esteem is often ignored because it and its related concepts can be somewhat confusing and complex. Let's disentangle some of this confusion by clarifying concepts that are related to self-esteem.

## *Identity*

Identity answers the questions: "Who am I? What defines me and my essential character?" Identity provides a sense of oneself and one's individuality (e.g., a woman's identity derived only from her role as a wife; a paraplegic's identity defined, not by a crippled body, but by the real or inner self).

## *Appreciate*

To think well of, to value, and to enjoy; to recognize gratefully; to *rightly* estimate the quality or worth of someone or something.

## *Accept*

To receive (i.e., to take in as one's own) favorably and with pleasure; approve; believe in; respond to favorably. *Self-acceptance* is believing in oneself, and receiving oneself favorably and with pleasure. One may accurately acknowledge one's weaknesses, be determined to improve, and still accept oneself. The internal dialogue might be, "I acknowledge my faults. I love myself, though not necessarily all of my behaviors. As I improve my behavior, then I can feel good about me *and* my behavior."

## *Self-Confidence*

Usually refers to a belief in one's abilities; related to competence and self-efficacy. As one's competence increases, one's confidence increases. In the broader and deeper sense, *self-confidence* is a belief in oneself as a person, leading to a general sense of "I can do it." Self-confident people might say to themselves: "Because anyone can do just about anything—given the time, practice, experience, resources, etc.—why can't I? I may not succeed completely or quickly, but the direction will be desirable." Demonstrating competence is satisfying, but it is an outgrowth of self-worth, not a way to establish it.

Competence and confidence correlate with self-esteem, but are not causal. If we base feelings of worth on competence and achievements, then if we fail there is no worth.

## *Pride*

English minister Charles Caleb Colton (1780–1832) wrote: "Pride makes some men ridiculous but prevents others from being so." There are two sides to pride as it relates to self-esteem: self-defeating and healthy.

As discussed previously, *self-defeating pride* is the attitude that one is superior, more valuable, or more important as a person than others. Such people also perceive themselves as more capable, self-sufficient, or infallible than they actually are. Synonyms for self-defeating pride include: haughtiness, arrogance, conceit, pretentiousness (i.e., trying to impress), vanity (i.e., excessive desire or need to be admired), narcissism (i.e., selfish; grandiose sense of self; exploitive). Self-defeating pride is typically rooted in fear (as in fear of being vulnerable) and/or the need to defend oneself.

*Healthy pride* is a realistic sense of one's own dignity or worth; self-respect; gratitude and delight in one's achievements, talents, service, or membership (i.e., in family, race, etc.).

### *Humility*

There also are two sides to humility: self-defeating humility and healthy humility. *Self-defeating humility* is an abject lack of self-respect (e.g., "dust of the earth"); spineless submissiveness; and contemptibility.

*Healthy humility*, on the other hand, involves an absence of self-defeating pride; the recognition of one's imperfections or weaknesses; consciousness of one's own shortcomings and ignorance; teachable. It is the realization that all are of equal worth. Healthy humility relates to meek behavior (in the positive sense), meaning mild, patient, and not easily stirred to anger.

Healthy humility and healthy pride coexist in the person with self-esteem. Humility because one realizes how much one still has to learn; pride in recognizing the dignity and worth one shares with all other humans.

The following amusing story (De Mello 1990) relates to one lacking in healthy humility:

> A guru advised a scholar: "Go out in the rain and raise your arms upward. That'll bring you a revelation."
>
> The next day the scholar reported back. "When I followed your advice, water flowed down my neck," he told the guru. "I felt like a complete fool."
>
> "For the first day, that's quite a revelation," replied the guru.

### *Selfishness*

Some mistakenly equate selfishness with self-esteem. So let's state an important principle: The purpose of self-esteem is to transcend the self. Self-consciousness is a painful situation that keeps one's focus inward. Healing the pain with love enables one's focus to expand outward, making one freer to love others and enjoy life. The person with self-esteem loves by choice from a secure base (as opposed, say, to a codependent individual who possesses neither self-esteem nor choice). Thus, building self-esteem warrants our best efforts.

## Cost/Benefits Analysis

Some people do not build self-esteem because they don't know how. But others resist building self-esteem, as difficult as that may be to believe, because there are apparent advantages to self-dislike. Before investing the time to build self-esteem, let's do what an effective manager would do before considering a new plan: a cost/benefits analysis. First, list all of the advantages of self-dislike you can think of. When you are finished, list all of the disadvantages. Some examples follow, and then there is a space for you to fill in a list of your own.

### *Examples of Advantages for Self-Dislike*

- No risk. I have no expectations of myself, nor do others. I can be lazy and set low goals. I'll rarely disappoint myself or others.
- The world is predictable. I understand when people don't accept me because I don't accept myself. I understand not having to try.
- Sometimes I get pity and attention, at least initially.
- Self-dislike is a family norm. When I follow the pattern, I feel like I fit in.

- Self-dislike keeps me from developing self-defeating pride.
- It justifies my poor dressing/grooming habits.

### *Examples of Disadvantages of Self-Dislike*

- It is very painful.
- Life is no fun.
- It leads to psychosomatic symptoms and disease.
- It creates a vicious cycle: Because I have a low opinion of myself, I don't try. Then others treat me poorly. They interpret my pessimism and apathy as indicators of incompetence. Their poor treatment of me confirms my low opinion of myself.

### *Your Personal Advantages and Disadvantages*

| **Pros/Advantages**<br>(The good thing about self-dislike is . . .) | **Cons/Disadvantages**<br>(The bad thing about self-dislike is . . .) |
| --- | --- |

### *Benefits of Emotional Change*

This analysis raises some very important questions. The ultimate question, of course, is: Is self-dislike a problem for me in terms of emotional, physical, or social costs? Others are: Are there ways to build self-esteem and still get my desires for attention, help, security, etc., met? Am I willing to risk losing some of the payoffs of self-dislike in order to get the gains of self-esteem? Progress is likely to begin as soon as one decides to count the cost of growth and pay its price.

Some find it helpful to test the waters before beginning to change. Try answering the question: What would be the positive consequences of my having a realistic and appreciative opinion of myself?

Some sample responses include:

- I'd be less susceptible to persuasion.
- I'd be less driven by fear.
- I'd be more motivated by enjoyment and personal satisfaction.
- I'd be happier.

- I'd try/risk more.
- I'd be more at ease with my rough edges and more willing to work on them.
- I'd be happier with my relationships and less likely to stick with partners who aren't worth it.
- I'd be more comfortable with expressing my feelings.
- I'd be less selfish and self-protecting.
- I'd be less questioning of myself and my actions when things go wrong.
- I'd worry less.
- I'd be more likely to be respected and treated well.
- I'd be considered more attractive.
- I'd enjoy life more.
- I'd make better, more objective decisions.
- I'd feel liked for who I am, and not for some phony person I wish I were.

Write your answers below:

## How to Build Self-Esteem

To change self-esteem is to first understand the factors on which it is built. Self-esteem is based on three sequential factors: (1) unconditional human worth, (2) love, and (3) growing.

### The Foundations of Self-Esteem

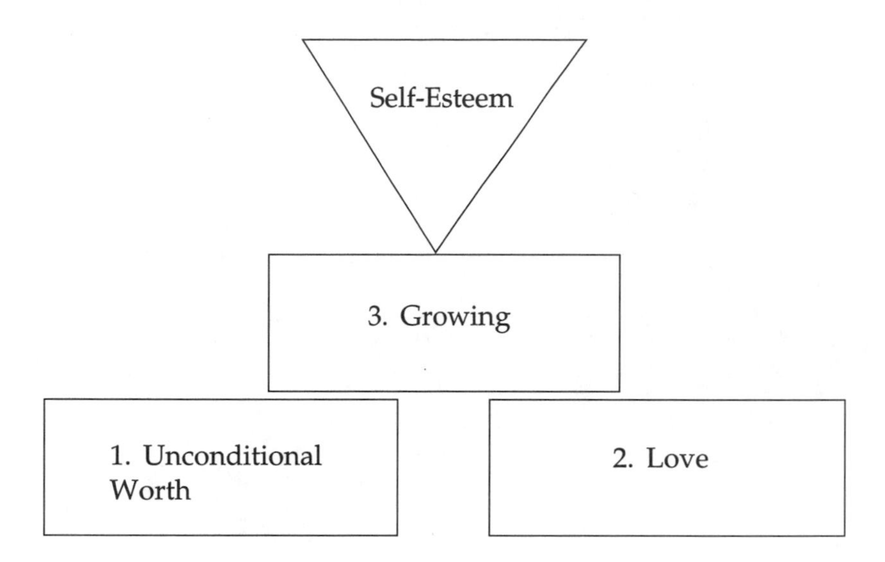


While all three factors are essential in building self-esteem, the *sequence* is crucial. Self-esteem is based first on unconditional worth, then love, and then growing. "Growing" (or "coming to flower") refers to moving in the desired direction. Too many people become frustrated because they try to start with growth, and neglect the first two important factors: unconditional worth and love. Without a secure base, self-esteem topples. The process cannot be short-circuited.

The remainder of this book deals sequentially with building the skills necessary to master each of the essential factors of building healthy self-esteem: the section called Factor I in Part II focuses on unconditional human worth, Factor II addresses love, and Factor III focuses on growing.

# Part II

## Factor I

# The Reality of Unconditional Human Worth

# Chapter 4

# The Basics of Human Worth

*Unconditional human worth* means that you are important and valuable as a person because your essential, core self is unique, precious, of infinite, eternal, unchanging value, and good. Unconditional human worth implies that you are as precious as any other person.

## Howard's Laws of Human Worth

Unconditional human worth is beautifully described by five axioms, which I call Howard's Laws, based on the work of Claudia A. Howard (1992).

1. All have infinite, internal, eternal, and unconditional worth *as persons.*
2. All have equal worth as people. Worth is not comparative or competitive. Although you might be better at sports, academics, or business, and I might be better in social skills, we both have equal worth as human beings.
3. Externals neither add to nor diminish worth. Externals include things like money, looks, performance, and achievements. These only increase one's *market* or *social* worth. Worth as a person, however, is infinite and unchanging.

4. Worth is stable and never in jeopardy (even if someone rejects you).
5. Worth doesn't have to be earned or proved. It already exists. Just recognize, accept, and appreciate it.

## The Core Self

The *human core,* sometimes called the essential, spiritual self, is like the European crystal, whose facets so beautifully reflect the sunlight.

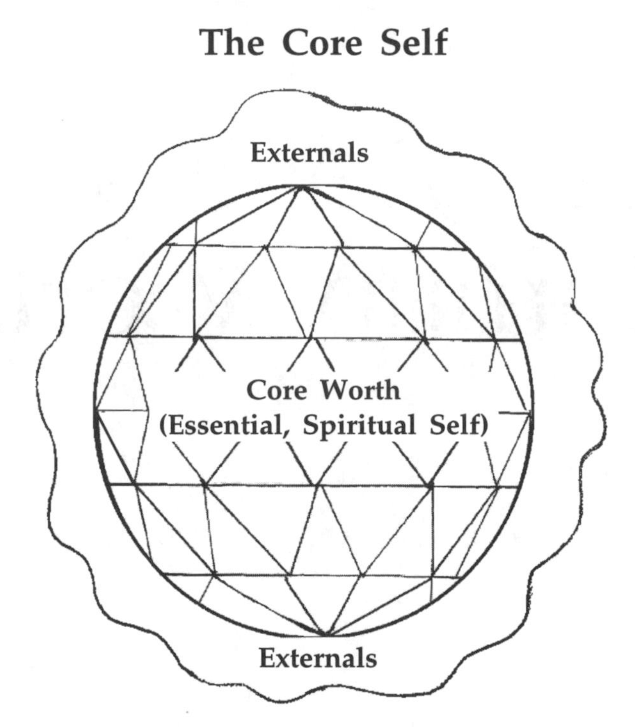


Much like a newborn baby, the core is fundamentally right and whole—complete, but not completed. *Completed* means fully developed and finished. A person is *complete* in the sense that each has every attribute, in embryo, that everyone else has—every attribute that is needed. The core is beautiful, lovable, and full of potential. The inner quality of the core self is demonstrated by this anecdote told by George Durrant (1980), a kind and loving teacher.

> One man was wrestling on the floor with his children and he decided he was tired so he faked like he was dead. That's one way you can get a rest. And the little boys were very concerned and one was a little older than the other and pried open his daddy's eye and he said to his little brother with some reassurance, "He's still *in* there."

What's *in* there is the core self. Over time, the core becomes surrounded with externals. Like a dirty film, some externals can hide the core. Other externals, like a halo, can brighten the core and allow its light to be seen or experienced. For example, mistakes or criticism may camouflage the core, making it difficult for one to see and experience one's worth. The love of others helps us feel our worth. A talent shared is one way to express worth. These change the way worth is experienced, not the worth itself.

Some spend their lives trying to look good on the outside to cover up shame, or a feeling of worthlessness, on the inside. If, however, we use externals to fill the empty feeling at the core, we will remain unfulfilled, perhaps always seeking approval, perhaps becoming cynical. Psychiatrists tell us that their offices are filled with people who ask, "Doctor, I am successful. Why am I unhappy?"

It is impossible to earn core worth through personal performance or any other external. It already exists. Consider the following list of externals.

## Worth As a Person Is Independent of Externals

Energy level
Appearance/Looks
Strength
Intelligence
Education
Gender
Race/Ethnicity/Skin color
Scholastic achievement/Grades
Skills
Friendliness
Talents
Creative ability
Handicaps
Material advantages
Wealth
Mistakes
Behavior
Decisions
Positions, Status
Physical fitness
Manners
Net/Market worth
Voice
Clothes
Car
Spirituality
Church activity
Worthiness
Blessings
Family image
Parents' status or character
Personality traits
Marriage status
Dates
Power
Being right
State of the economy/stock market
Inexperience

**Present Functioning Level**

Attitudes
Daily self-evaluations
Performance
Hygiene/Grooming
Sickness/Health
Productivity
Resilience
Confidence
Control over events
Selfishness or selflessness
Feelings

**Comparisons**

Competence relative to others
(e.g., in sports, salary)

**Judgments of Others**

How many people like you
Others' approval or acceptance
How others treat you

## *Illustrative Examples*

The person with self-esteem beholds and appreciates the core self. This person sees flaws as external to the core, which require attention, developing, nurturing, and/or acceptance when change is not possible. The following four examples illustrate the idea of core worth.

### A Spirited Young Boy

I take courage from a spirited young boy's example. Confined to a wheelchair, he matter-of-factly explained, "A tumor broke the nerve that tells my legs what to do." He knew how to separate worth from externals.

### A Former Student

Another who radiated a quiet inner gladness is Ken Kirk, a former student of mine. He created this poem:

**If I Could Be**

If I could be a tree I would
provide shade for all mankind.

If I could be the sea I would
be calm for all to travel.

If I could be the sun I would
provide warmth for all living things.

If I could be the wind I would
be a cool breeze on a hot summer day.

If I could be the rain I would
keep the earth fertile.

But, to be any one of these things would be to miss out on all the rest. And this is why,
if I could be anything I would be nothing more than me.

—Ken Kirk, student

### The State of Virginia

The state of Virginia has several beautiful colonial bed and breakfast inns. Staying in one with a lovely stone fireplace, I beheld an antique wooden duck. Large, plain, unpainted, carved perhaps by a colonial farmer, it added a simple touch of class to the homey room. Near the fireplace was a large log, which was appreciated because the night was chilly. I asked my students which has more worth, the wooden duck or the wooden log? One woman thoughtfully answered, "Their worth is the same. They are just different."

### Through the Eyes of a Schoolteacher

A friend, a schoolteacher, was in a bus with her students. The bus was struck by another bus, resulting in a number of injuries. Afterward, she reflected, "After the accident, I watched the children running around assuming leadership and caring for each other, and then I could truly see their worth." Events can help us to *see* worth, but they neither add to nor diminish core worth.

## Separating Worth from Externals

This is the goal: Separate core worth from externals.

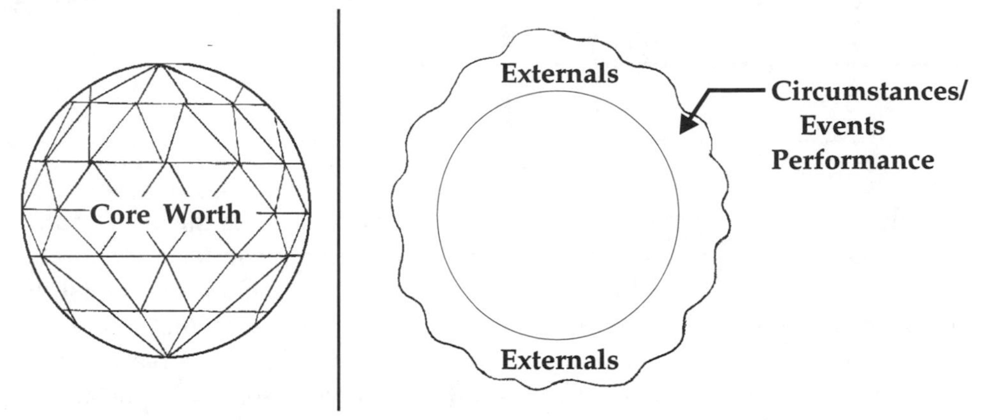


Used by permission Claudia A. Howard, Individual Potential Seminars, as are the next two diagrams.

The goal of separating worth from externals can be difficult in today's culture. The emphasis of today's television programming can convey the message that you are not worthwhile if you are not young, bold, beautiful, or wealthy. Fast-lane living in today's cities conveys the message that you must be high powered and successful to be somebody. Taken to the unrestrained extreme, today's work ethic can suggest that one loses worth if one is sleeping, vacationing, or not producing.

Let's consider two ways to look at human worth: Proposition one: Worth equals externals. Proposition two: Worth is separate from externals.

### *When Worth Equals Externals*

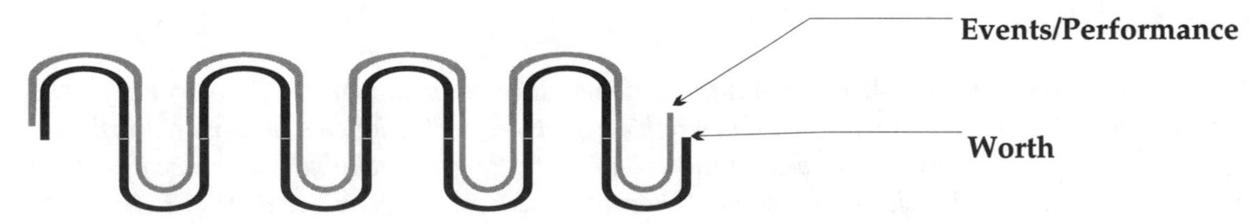


When worth equals externals, self-esteem rises and falls along with events. For instance, a high school student explained that she feels less worthwhile when she looks in the mirror and notices her complexion. Then she feels better when that cute guy says hello; when he fails to ask her for a date, she feels depressed. A compliment on her dress, she feels great; a math exam, she feels bad. She feels great when she and that guy begin dating, miserable when they break up. She is on an emotional roller coaster.

For adults, the highs may come with promotions, awards, or entrance to medical school. The lows may come with criticism, poor performance, or when your team loses.

If your worth equals your job or your marriage, how will you feel if you realize you have already gotten your last promotion or if you divorce? Your feelings would probably go beyond the normal and appropriate sadness and disappointment. When worth is in doubt, depression usually follows. If human worth equals market worth, then only the rich and powerful have worth. By this line of thinking, a Donald Trump or Hitler would have more human worth than a Mother Teresa.

*When Worth Is Separate from Externals*

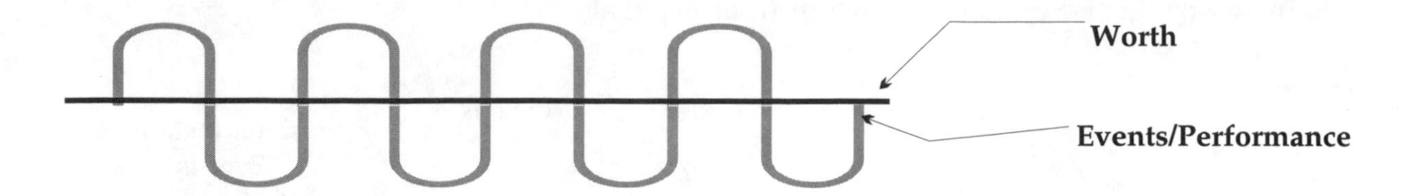


When worth is separate from externals, human worth is intrinsic and unchanging, irrespective of outside events or circumstances. Here, we distinguish feeling bad about events or behaviors (guilt) from feeling bad about the core self (shame). Guilt for foolish behavior is a healthy motivation for change. Condemning the core, however, saps motivation.

The idea is to judge behavior, but not the core. One can be reasonably objective in judging behaviors and present skill levels. It is difficult to be reasonable or objective when one has condemned the self at the core.

It is also wise to separate uncomfortable feelings arising from disappointment, illness, fatigue, chemical fluctuations, anger, anxiety, etc., from feeling bad about the core self.

Let's take an example of a difficult situation. Say that a promotion you desired was awarded to someone else. You tell yourself, "Perhaps some of my skills are not up to par yet for this job." This is a statement of fact that judges your skill level, experience, or training. This would result in appropriate disappointment and perhaps the decision to improve your skills. On the other hand, if you told yourself, "I'm not good enough as a person," this is a statement of worth that means you are inferior as a person. Obviously, this self-destructive choice of thoughts would lead to self-dislike and perhaps depression. So judge your present skills and performance, never the core.

## Why Individuals Have Worth

*I dedicate this section to people who struggle with the notion of unconditional worth. I think of a man who was attending a self-esteem class. Intellectual and bright, he listened to the axioms of human worth. He was struggling, looking like he wanted to believe them, but unable to grasp why all human beings could have worth, despite their imperfections and foolish behaviors. The light went on eventually, to his great pleasure.*

I'd like to start by posing some questions: Why do people spend millions of dollars to extricate from a well a two-year-old girl who has never done anything of note? Why do we love a baby? How are we like a dog or an inanimate object? How are we different?

A human has worth for at least four reasons:

1. *Present endowments.* A human's innate nature is enjoyable. It is fun to watch a child play in the leaves or respond to the beauty of nature. It is fun to love children and see them respond with a smile, joy, a sense of play, affection, or the security to take on the world with enthusiasm.

2. *Capacities.* When people behave obnoxiously, it is fun to ponder their potential to beautify life with art, craftsmanship, or other creations; with emotions of pleasure, acceptance, and encouragement; with laughter, work, and love. Capacities are innate, and able to be discovered and developed. When we err, we have the capacity to correct our course. Thus, we observe that human beings are fallible but infinitely perfectible and have an

"ability to convert not just their food, but also their hopes, into vital energy" (Cousins 1983). When theologians point to the notion that humans are created in God's image and likeness, they refer to the concept that a person is like a seed—whole; complete, but not completed—possessing in embryo every conceivable capacity: to think rationally, to emote, to sacrifice, to love, to make ethical choices, to recognize truth and worth, to create, to beautify, to be gentle, patient, or firm.

3. *Past contributions.* If one ever contributed to the well-being of others or self—in any way, large or small—then that person is not worthless.

4. *The craftsmanship of the body.* Although it is an external, the body is a nice metaphor for the core self. A number of influences in today's culture tend to "thing-ify" the body. The media glorifies using others as pleasure objects. Many individuals have been sexually or physically abused. When a body is mistreated, a person can come to see the body as disgusting. The greater danger is that they will come to devalue the core self. On the other hand, considering the marvelous intricacies of the body with respect can help a person appreciate the worth of the core self. (We shall return to this important concept in chapters 15 and 16.)

Sometimes people ask, "What if I am ugly or crippled—how can I feel worthwhile?" I challenge them to pretend they are crippled and to come up with ways by which they could still assert and experience their worth. The responses are often illuminating:

- I could convey love through my eyes
- I could learn to allow people to help me and to enjoy their service
- I could change my thoughts; I could learn to define myself as more than my body
- I could demonstrate my will (e.g., by appreciating what I see, by trying to move even a finger, by improving my mind)

We repeatedly return to the underlying concepts. Worth is already there. It is there whether you are sleeping or producing. The core is more than behavior, position, or any other external. Our challenge is to experience and enjoy that core worth.

Worth is neither comparative nor competitive, as is demonstrated by the experience of this father:

> Three of my children were swinging at a park and two of them had learned to pump themselves in the swing and that's always a happy day for a father when his children learn to pump themselves in a swing. And two of them were going real high and Devon says, "I'm keeping up with Katherine," and Katherine looked across and said, "I'm keeping up with Devon" 'cause they were swinging right together. And little Marinda was in the middle and she was just barely moving because there was a breeze. And little Marinda, hearing them saying they're keeping up with each other . . . said, "I'm just keeping up with myself" (Durrant 1980).

Even at a young age, a child can understand the concept of intrinsic worth that is not comparative or competitive, and will be better off for it.

## Reflections on Unconditional and Equal Human Worth

Please ponder the reflections on human worth below. When you finish you'll be ready to begin the human worth skill building activities, which are found in chapters 5 through 9.

*We (are) equal inhabitants of a paradise of individuals in which everybody has the right to be understood.*

—Richard Rorty (1991)

*We hold these truths to be self-evident, that all men are created equal, that they are endowed by their Creator with certain unalienable rights, that among those are life, liberty, and the pursuit of happiness.*

—The Declaration of Independence, July 4, 1776

*We are all basically the same human beings, who seek happiness and try to avoid suffering.*

*Everybody is my peer group.*

*Your feeling "I am of no value" is wrong. Absolutely wrong.*

—The Dalai Lama

*You're as good as anybody.*

—Spoken to Martin Luther King by his father.

*All men are alike when asleep.*

—Aristotle

*(We) are made in the image of God—a good God, a God of beauty . . . God declared his creation good.*

—Rebecca Manley Pippert (1999)

*We need to see ourselves as basic miracles.*

—Virginia Satir

*Men can be human, with human frailties, and still be great.*

—Stephen L. Richards (1955)

*Heroes don't need lettermen jackets. We know who we are.*

—Evil Knievel

*Letting circumstances or others determine worth*
*gives them inappropriate control and power.*

—Anonymous

*When our value as human beings depends on what we make with*
*our hands and minds, we become victims of the fear tactics of*
*our world. When productivity is our main way of overcoming*
*self-doubt, we are extremely vulnerable to rejection and criticism*
*and prone to inner anxiety and depression.*

—Henry J. M. Nouwen (1989)

*Problems are weaknesses (which respond to strengthening),*
*not illnesses (which need removal of causal agents).*

—William Glasser

*Every cliché you've ever heard about babies is true, it seems to me.*
*They are soft and warm, fascinating, cute, and lovable. I never met*
*one that wasn't, and it's a good thing too, because if babies weren't*
*so cute and lovable maybe we wouldn't so gladly put up with*
*the fact that they're so demanding and so much trouble.*

*Babies are pure potential. You pick up a little baby and you're*
*amazed by how light it is, but you feel also that you're holding the*
*future, the earth and the sky, the sun and the moon, and all*
*of it, everything, is brand new.*

*Babies help us to put the changing world into perspective too.*
*Changing the world has to wait, when it's time to change the baby.*

—Charles Osgood

Chapter 5

# Recognize and Replace Self-Defeating Thoughts

Although all humans are infinitely worthwhile, all do not necessarily have a sense of their own worth. One reason is that negative, depressing thought patterns can erode one's sense of worth. Note: We're not saying that worth is eroded, only one's ability to experience it.

Consider this situation. The boss scowls as he passes John and Bill in the hall. John begins to feel down on himself as he thinks, "Oh, no! He's upset with me." Bill only gets concerned, not disturbed, as he tells himself, "The boss is probably having another battle with the front office." What is the difference between the two? Not the event, but the way John and Bill thought about the event.

A branch of psychology called cognitive therapy has identified specific thought patterns that attack self-esteem and lead to depression. These thought patterns have been learned. They can be unlearned. Cognitive therapy provides an effective, straightforward way to eliminate these self-destructive thoughts and replace them with more reasonable thoughts. The model, developed by psychologist Albert Ellis, is simple:

A ——————————→ B ——————————→ C

A stands for the Activating (or upsetting) event. B is the Belief (or automatic thoughts) that we tell ourselves about A. C is the emotional Consequences (or feelings, such as worthlessness or depression). Most people think A causes C. In reality, it is B, our self-talk, that has the greater influence.

## Automatic Thoughts and Distortions

Whenever an upsetting event occurs, automatic thoughts (ATs) run through our minds. Although we're each capable of thinking reasonably about upsetting events, sometimes our automatic thoughts are distorted—or unreasonably negative. Distorted ATs occur so rapidly that we hardly notice them, let alone stop to question them. Yet these ATs profoundly affect our moods and our sense of worth. In this section, you'll learn to catch these distortions, challenge their logic, and replace them with thoughts that more closely align with reality instead of thoughts that depress.

The distortions fall into only thirteen categories. Learn them well. Using them will be a very powerful tool in building self-esteem.

### *Assuming*

In these circumstances, we assume the worst without testing the evidence. For instance, in the example above John assumed that the boss' scowl meant he was angry with John. John could have tested this assumption by simply asking, "Boss, are you angry with me?"

Assuming self-talk would also be when you tell yourself, "I know I won't enjoy myself," or "I know I'll do a lousy job even though I'm prepared." More reasonable self-talk would be: "I might or might not enjoy myself (do a good job, etc.). I'm willing to experiment and see what happens."

### *Shoulds (Musts/Oughts)*

Shoulds (musts/oughts) are demands we make of ourselves. For example: "I should be a perfect lover"; "I must not make mistakes"; "I should have known better"; or "I should be happy and never depressed or tired." We think that we motivate ourselves with such statements. Usually, however, we just feel worse (e.g., since I *should* be so and so, and I'm not that way, I then feel inadequate, frustrated, ashamed, and hopeless).

Perhaps one of the only reasonable "shoulds" is that humans "should" be fallible, just as we are, given our background, our imperfect understanding, and our present skill levels. If we *really* knew better (i.e., if we clearly understood the advantages of certain behaviors, and were perfectly capable of behaving that way), then we *would* be better. One solution, then, is to replace "shoulds" with "woulds" or "coulds" (It *would* be nice if I did that. I wonder how I *could* do that). Or replace "shoulds" with "want to's" (I *want to* do that because it is to my advantage, not because someone is telling me I *should* or *must*).

## *The Fairy-Tale Fantasy*

The fairy-tale fantasy means demanding the ideal from life. This is really a special type of "should." "That's not fair!" or "Why did that have to happen?" often means "The world shouldn't be the way it is." In reality, bad and unfair things happen to good people—sometimes randomly, sometimes because of the unreasonableness of others, and sometimes because of our own imperfections. To expect that the world be different is to invite disappointment. To expect that others treat us fairly, when they often have their own ideas about what is fair, is also to invite disappointment. Again, a "would" or a "could" is a wise substitute for a "should" (e.g., "It *would* be nice if things were ideal, but they're not. Too bad. Now, I wonder what I *could* do to improve things").

## *All or Nothing Thinking*

With all or nothing thinking you hold yourself to the impossible standard of perfection (or something close to it). When you fall short of this standard, you conclude that you are a total failure as a person. For example, "If I'm not the best, I'm a flop"; "If I'm not performing perfectly, I'm a loser"; "If I score below 90 percent, I am a failure"; "A rough edge means I'm all bad." This is unreasonable because such absolute, black and white extremes rarely exist. Even if it were possible to perform perfectly (it isn't), performing below some standard usually means we've performed at 80 percent or 35 percent—rarely at 0 percent. And poor *performance* never makes a complex *person* worthless, just fallible. Ask yourself, "Why *must* I bat one thousand?"

## *Overgeneralizing*

Overgeneralizing is deciding that negative experiences describe your life completely. For example, "I *always* ruin *everything*"; "I *always* get rejected in love"; "*No one* likes me; *everybody* hates me"; "I *never* do well at math." Such global statements are unkind, depressing, and usually inaccurate to some degree. The antidote is to use more precise language: "*Some* of my skills are not *yet* well developed"; "I'm not as tactful in *some* social situations as I'd like"; "*Sometimes* people don't approve of me (*sometimes some* people do)"; "Although *some* aspects of my life haven't gone well, that doesn't mean I never do reasonably well." Be a healthy optimist: expect to find small ways to improve situations and notice what's going well.

## *Labeling*

Here you give yourself a label, or name, as though a single word describes a person completely. For example: "I'm such a loser"; "I'm stupid"; "I'm dumb"; "I'm boring." To say, "I *am* stupid" means I *always*, in every way, am stupid. In fact, some people who behave quite stupidly at times, also behave quite intelligently at other times. Because humans are too complex for simple labels, confine labels to behaviors (e.g., "That was a silly thing to do."), or ask, "Am I *always* stupid? Sometimes, perhaps, but not *always*."

## *Dwelling on the Negative*

Suppose you go to a party and notice that a guest has dog poop on his shoe. The more you think about it, the more uncomfortable you get. In this distortion, you focus in on the negative aspects of a situation, while ignoring the positive aspects. Soon the whole situation looks negative. Other examples: "How can I feel good about the day when I was criticized?"; "How can I enjoy life when my children have problems?"; "How can I feel good about myself when I make mistakes?"; "The steak is burnt—the meal is ruined!" A solution to this habit is to re-examine your options: "Would I enjoy things more (and feel better about myself) if I chose a different focus?"; "What pleasing things could I still find to enjoy?"; "What would I think on a good day?"; "How would someone with sound self-esteem view this situation?"

### *Rejecting the Positive*

Dwelling on the negative overlooks positive aspects. Here we actually negate positives so that our self-esteem remains low. For example, someone compliments your work. You reply, "Oh, it was really nothing. Anyone could do that." You discount the fact that you've worked long and effectively. No wonder accomplishments aren't fun. You could just as easily have replied, "Thanks" (and tell yourself, "I do deserve special credit for doing this difficult and boring task"). You would give a loved one or friend credit where it's due. Why not do yourself the same favor?

### *Unfavorable Comparisons*

Suppose you had an unusual magnifying glass that magnified some things (like your faults and mistakes, or the strengths of others) and shrunk others (like your strengths, and the mistakes of others). In comparison to others, you would always seem inadequate or inferior—always coming out on the short end of the stick.

For example, you think to yourself: "I'm only a housewife and mother" (minimizing your strengths). "Jan's a rich, bright lawyer" (magnifying another's strengths). Your friend replies: "But you're an excellent homemaker. You've been great with your kids. Jan's an alcoholic." To which you respond: "Yes, but (minimizing another's faults and your accomplishments) look at the cases she's won! She's the one who really contributes! (Magnifying another's strengths.)"

A way to challenge this distortion is to ask, "Why must I compare? Why can't I just appreciate that each person has unique strengths and weaknesses? Another's contributions are not necessarily better, just different."

### *Catastrophizing*

When you believe that something is a catastrophe, you tell yourself that it is so horrible and awful that "I can't stand it!" In telling ourselves this, we convince ourselves that we are too feeble to cope with life. For example, "I couldn't stand it if she were to leave me. It would be awful!" Although many things are unpleasant, inconvenient, and difficult, we can really stand anything short of being steamrolled to death, as Albert Ellis has said. So one might think, "I didn't like this, but I certainly *can* stand it."

Asking the following questions will challenge the belief that something will be a catastrophe:

- What are the odds of this happening?
- If it does happen, how likely is it to do me in?
- If the worst happens, what will I do? (Anticipating a problem and formulating an action plan increases one's sense of confidence.)

- One hundred years from now, will anyone care about this?

## *Personalizing*

Personalizing is seeing yourself as more involved in negative events than you really are. For example, a student drops out of college and the mother concludes, "It's all my fault." A husband takes full responsibility for his spouse's fatigue or anger, or for a divorce. Here the ego is so involved that each event becomes a test of worth. There are two helpful antidotes to this distortion:

- Distinguish *influences* from *causes*. Sometimes we can influence others' decisions, but the final decision is theirs, not ours.
- Look realistically for other influences outside of ourselves. For example, instead of thinking, "What's wrong with me? Why can't I do this?" one might say, "This is a difficult task. The help I need isn't here, it's noisy, and I'm tired." Instead of thinking, "Why is he snapping at me?" one might say, "Maybe I'm not the central character. Maybe he's mad at the world today."

## *Blaming*

Blaming is the opposite of personalizing. Whereas personalizing puts all the responsibility on yourself for your difficulties, blaming puts it all on something outside of yourself. For example:

- He make's me so mad!
- She has ruined my life and my self-esteem.
- I am a loser because of my crummy childhood.

The problem with blaming, much like catastrophizing, is that it tends to make us think of ourselves as helpless victims who are too powerless to cope. The antidote to blaming is to acknowledge outside influences, but to take responsibility for your own welfare: "Yes, his behavior was unjust and unfair, but I don't have to turn bitter and cynical. I am better than that."

Notice that the person with self-esteem is free to assume realistic responsibility. He will acknowledge what *is* his responsibility and what is *not*. However, when one takes responsibility, it is for a behavior or a choice, not for being bad to the core. Thus, one might say, "I performed poorly on that exam because I did not study enough. Next time I'll plan better." There is no judging the core self here, only behaviors.

## *Making Feelings Facts*

Making feelings facts is taking one's feelings as proof of the way things really are. For example:

- I feel like such a loser. I must be hopeless.
- I feel ashamed and bad. I must be bad.
- I feel inadequate. I must be inadequate.
- I feel worthless. I must be worthless.

Remember that feelings result from our thoughts. If our thoughts are distorted (as they often are when we're stressed or depressed), then our feelings may not reflect reality. So question your feelings. Ask, "What would someone who is 100 percent inadequate (or bad, guilty, hopeless, etc.) be like? Am I really like that?" This challenges the tendencies of labeling or all or nothing thinking. Remind yourself that feelings are not facts. When our thoughts become more reasonable, our feelings become brighter.

## The Daily Thought Record

Now that you know about distortions, the next step is to use them to help you with your self-esteem . When we're stressed or depressed, thoughts and feelings can swirl in our minds and seem overwhelming. Putting them down on paper helps us sort it all out and see things more clearly. The Daily Thought Record (on the following pages) takes about fifteen minutes each day. It is good to do it after you notice yourself feeling upset. Or it can be done later in the day, when things calm down. Here's how it works:

### *The Facts*

At the top of the record briefly describe an upsetting event and the resulting feelings (sad, anxious, guilty, frustrated, etc.). Rate the intensity of these feelings (10 means extremely unpleasant). Remember, getting in touch with disturbing feelings is a way to stop them from controlling us.

### *Analysis of Your Thoughts*

In the first column of the Analysis Section, list your Automatic Thoughts (ATs). Then rate how much you believe each. 10 means it's completely believable.

In the second column, identify the distortions (some ATs might be rational).

In the third column, try to respond, or talk back, to each distorted AT. Realize that your first AT is only one of several possible choices. Try to imagine what you would say to a friend who said what you did, or try to imagine yourself on a good day saying something more reasonable. Ask yourself, "What is the evidence for the reasonable response?" Then rate how much you believe each response.

### *Results*

After all this, go back to the Initial Responses column and rerate your ATs. Then at the top rerate the intensity of your emotions. If the process leads to even a slight drop in your upset feelings, feel satisfied. With this process, upsetting events will still probably be upsetting, just not as disturbing.

Remember, work out your thoughts on paper. It is too complex to do it in your head. Be patient with yourself as you learn how to do this. It usually takes a few weeks to become good at this skill.

Each day for the next two weeks, select an upsetting event and do a Daily Thought Record. At the end of the two weeks, proceed to the next section, Getting to the Bottom of Things.

# Daily Thought Record

## The Facts

| **Event** (Describe the event that "made you" feel bad/unpleasant) | **Impact of Event** (Describe the emotions you felt) | **Intensity** (Rate the intensity of these emotions from 1–10) |
|---|---|---|
| | | |

## Analysis of Your Thoughts

| **Initial Responses** (Describe the Automatic Thoughts or Self-Talk. Then rate how believable each is from 1–10) | | **Thought Fallacies** (Find and label the distortions) | **Reasonable Resonses** (Talk back! Change the distortions to more reasonable thoughts. Rate how much you believe each from 1–10) | |
|---|---|---|---|---|
| | Ratings | | | Ratings |
| | | | | |

## Results

Based upon your Thought Analysis, rerate how much you believe your initial responses. Then rerate the intensity of your emotions.

Here's an example of a simplified Daily Thought Record.

| Event | Impact | Intensity |
|---|---|---|
| Bill and I broke up | Depressed<br>Worthless | 9→6<br>8→5 |

## Analysis

| Automatic Thoughts | | Distortions | Reasonable Responses | |
|---|---|---|---|---|
| It's all my fault | 8→5 | Personalizing | We both made mistakes, even though we did as well as we were able | 8 |
| I feel so rejected. I'm worthless | 9→8 | Making Feelings Facts<br>Labeling | As long as I have ever, or could ever, make a difference to someone (including myself) I'm not worthless | 7 |
| He hates me | 7→3 | Assuming | He might just feel I'm not his cup of tea | 9 |
| I'll never find another as suitable | 10→8 | Assuming | I don't know that. It's possible that I could find someone more accepting and, therefore, more suitable | 7 |
| Without him nothing will be fun | 10→5 | Assuming | I won't know this unless I test it out. Probably there are things I could enjoy both alone and with others | 7 |
| That guy has ruined my life | 9→5 | Blaming | Nobody but me can ruin my life. I'll rebound from this and find ways to enjoy myself | 9 |

On the following page is another blank Daily Thought Record to practice on or to copy.

# Daily Thought Record

Date: ____________________

## The Facts

| **Event** (Describe the event that "made you" feel bad/unpleasant) | **Impact of Event** (Describe the emotions you felt) | **Intensity** (Rate the intensity of these emotions from 1–10) |
|---|---|---|
| | | |

## Analysis of Your Thoughts

| **Initial Responses** (Describe the Automatic Thoughts or Self-Talk. Then rate how believable each is from 1–10) | | **Thought Fallacies** (Find and label the distortions) | **Reasonable Resonses** (Talk back! Change the distortions to more reasonable thoughts. Rate how much you believe each from 1–10) | |
|---|---|---|---|---|
| | Ratings | | | Ratings |
| | | | | |

## Results

Based upon your Thought Analysis, rerate how much you believe your initial responses. Then rerate the intensity of your emotions.

## Getting to the Bottom of Things: The Question and Answer Technique

So far you have learned to use the Daily Thought Record to identify and replace distorted ATs. While replacing distorted ATs can strengthen self-esteem, uprooting core beliefs provides an even greater lift. Core beliefs are deeply held beliefs. Because they are usually learned early in life, they are rarely challenged. We discover core beliefs by starting with an AT and using the Question and Answer Technique. In this approach, you take an AT and until you reach the core belief you keep asking the following questions:

"What does this mean to me?"

Or

"Assuming that's true, why is that so bad?"

For example, on one Daily Thought Record, Jane has expressed a feeling of helplessness and worthlessness because her daughter refused to clean her room. Jane decided to apply the Question and Answer Technique to the AT: "The room is a mess." It went like this:

| | |
|---|---|
| *Automatic Thought:* | The room is a mess. |
| *Question:* | What does that mean to me? |
| *Answer:* | She's a slob! |
| *Question:* | Assuming that's true, why is that so bad? |
| *Answer:* | My friends will come over and see her messy room. |
| *Question:* | Why would that be so bad? |
| *Answer:* | They'll think I'm an inadequate mother. |
| *Question:* | Assuming that's true, why would that be so bad? |
| *Answer:* | I can't feel worthwhile if my friends disapprove of me. = CORE BELIEF! |

In reaching this core belief, you've assumed that each answer along the way is true. Now go back and look for distortions among your answers, responding reasonably at each step. The following shows what the whole process looks like, using the three columns from the Daily Thought Record. The "Q" represents questions, which need not be written down.

| Initial Responses (ATs) | Distortions | Reasonable Responses |
|---|---|---|
| This room is a mess | | |
| Q | | |
| She's a slob | Labeling | Actually she's quite neat in areas that matter to her, like her appearance |
| Q | | |
| My friends will come over and see her messy room | | Even if they do, lots of worthwhile people have daughters with sloppy rooms |
| Q | | |
| They'll think I'm an inadequate mother | Assuming<br>All-or-Nothing Thinking | They might just think I'm fallible, just like them |
| Q | | |
| I can't feel worthwhile if my friends disapprove of me | CORE BELIEF! | I don't have to be perfect or have everyone's approval to be happy, or to consider myself worthwhile. It *would* be nice if everything I did was beyond reproach. But since no one is perfect, I'd better decide to feel worthwhile anyway |

## Some Common Core Beliefs

Research has found that a number of core beliefs identified by the psychologist Albert Ellis are consistently linked to self-dislike and depression. These deserve special mention, along with their rational replacements (Bourne 1992):

1. Core Belief: *I must be loved or approved by everyone I consider significant.*

   Rational response: I want to be loved or approved by most people, and I will try to act in a respectful manner so they will. But it is inevitable that some people, for their own reasons, will not like or accept me. This is not catastrophic; my self-esteem can't depend on the whims of others.

2. Core Belief: *I must be thoroughly competent and adequate in everything I do. I should not be satisfied with myself unless I'm the best or excelling.*

   Rational response: I will strive to do *my* best rather than to be *the* best. I can enjoy doing things even if I'm not particularly good at them. I'm not afraid to try things where I might fail; I'm fallible, and failing does not mean I'm a lousy person. Rather, taking risks is courageous and is a necessity if I'm to grow and experience life's opportunities.

3. Core Belief: *If something is or may be dangerous or fearsome I must be terribly concerned about it and keep on guard in case it happens.*

   Rational response: It is probably in my best interest to face this thing and render it less dangerous, and, if that is impossible, I will stop dwelling on it and being fearful. Worry will not stop it from happening. Even if it happened I could cope with it.

4. Core Belief: *It is easier to avoid than face life's difficulties and responsibilities.*

   Rational response: I'll do those necessary things no matter how much I dislike them. Living is just that; resting and avoiding are often legitimate intervals in a full life, but they are counterproductive if they occupy the major part of my life.

Please note: The last two irrational beliefs address how we deal with worries. They are consistent with other research that shows that extremes are generally self-defeating. That is, both obsessing about worries and denying/avoiding them tend to have negative consequences. As a rule, the middle ground approach of *efficient* worry has the healthiest consequences: Focus on worries for a limited time, with a problem-solving approach. For a portion of the day (some research suggests about 30 minutes), gather facts, consider alternatives, acknowledge feelings, write or talk about your concerns, take appropriate action. After that, allow yourself to shift your focus to life's loveliness.

## Examining Unproductive Core Beliefs

Below is a list of commonly held, yet unproductive core beliefs. As an exercise, circle those that you hold. Then try to dispute them. You might further discuss rational responses with a respected friend or mental health professional.

1. It's bad to think well of myself.
2. I can't be happy unless a certain condition—like success, money, love, approval, or perfect achievement—is met.
3. I can't feel worthwhile unless a certain condition is met.
4. I'm entitled to happiness (or success, health, self-respect, pleasure, love) without having to work for it.
5. One day when I make it, I'll have friends and be able to enjoy myself.
6. Work should be hard and in some way unpleasant.
7. Joy is *only* gained from hard work.
8. I am inadequate.
9. Worrying insures that I'll be prepared to face and solve problems. So the more I worry the better. (Constant worrying helps prevent future mistakes and problems and gives me extra control.)
10. Life should be easy. I can't enjoy it if there are problems.
11. The past makes me unhappy. There's no way around it.
12. There's a perfect solution, and I must find it.
13. If people disapprove of (reject, criticize, mistreat) me, it means I'm inferior, wrong, or no good.
14. I'm only as good as the work I do. If I'm not productive, I'm no good.
15. If I try hard enough, all people will like me.
16. If I try hard enough, my future will be happy and trouble free.

17. Life must be fair.

Notice how many of these core beliefs directly affect self-esteem! Notice how many of these core beliefs make an external condition a requirement of worth or happiness. For one week, use the Question and Answer Technique once a day to find your core beliefs. Use previously completed Daily Thought Records, or a newly completed Thought Record.

Chapter 6

# Acknowledge Reality: "Nevertheless!"

Now that you have acquired the skill of recognizing and replacing self-defeating thoughts, you are ready for a skill that is quite a favorite among students of self-esteem. The appeal of this skill is that it helps one acknowledge reality and still feel good about one's core self.

First, let's review some key points:

1. Feeling bad about events, behaviors, outcomes, or some other external can be appropriate (as in appropriate guilt or disappointment). This is different from the unhealthy tendency to feel bad about the core self (previously described as shame).

2. Saying "I am not quite adequate for the job yet" is quite different from "I'm no good *as a person.*" Feeling bad about failing is very different from "I am a failure" at the core.

3. It's okay to judge your behaviors and skills, but not your core, essential self.

# A Skill-Building Activity

We want to acknowledge unpleasant external conditions without condemning the core self. People who dislike the self tend to use *Because . . . therefore* thoughts. For example, "*Because* of (some external condition), *therefore* I am no good as a person." Obviously, this thought will erode self-esteem and/or keep it from developing. So we want to avoid *Because . . . therefore* thoughts.

The *Nevertheless* skill provides a realistic, upbeat, immediate response to unpleasant externals—a response that reinforces one's sense of worth by separating worth from externals. Therefore, instead of a *Because . . . therefore* thought, we use an *Even though . . . nevertheless* thought. It looks like this:

*Even though* ___________________________ *nevertheless* ___________________________

(some external) (some statement of worth)

For example: "*Even though* I botched that project, *nevertheless* I'm still a worthwhile person." Other Nevertheless statements are:

- Nevertheless, I'm still of great worth
- Nevertheless, I'm still an important and valuable person
- Nevertheless, my worth is infinite and unchangeable

## *A "Nevertheless" Exercise*

Get a partner. Ask your partner to say whatever negative things come to mind, be they true or false, such as:

- You really blew it!
- You have a funny nose!
- You mumble when you talk!
- You bug me!
- You're a big dummy!

To each criticism, put your ego on the shelf, and respond with an *Even though . . . nevertheless* statement (Howard 1992). You'll probably want to use some of your cognitive therapy skills. For example, if someone labels you "a dummy," you could respond, "Even though I *behave* in dumb ways sometimes, nevertheless . . ." Author Jack Canfield (1988) is fond of a similar approach that even a five-year-old child can apply: "No matter what you do or say, I am still a worthwhile person."

## Skill-Building Worksheet

### *Steps*

1. For each of the next six days, select three events that have the potential to erode self-esteem.

2. In response to each event, create an *Even though . . . nevertheless* statement. Then describe below the event or situation, the statement used, and the effect on your feelings of selecting this statement and saying it to yourself. Keeping a written record reinforces the skill.

| Date | Event/Situation | Statement Used | Effect |
|---|---|---|---|
| Day One | | | |
| 1. | | | |
| 2. | | | |
| 3. | | | |
| Day Two | | | |
| 1. | | | |
| 2. | | | |
| 3. | | | |
| Day Three | | | |
| 1. | | | |
| 2. | | | |
| 3. | | | |
| Day Four | | | |
| 1. | | | |
| 2. | | | |
| 3. | | | |
| Day Five | | | |
| 1. | | | |
| 2. | | | |
| 3. | | | |
| Day Six | | | |
| 1. | | | |
| 2. | | | |
| 3. | | | |

## Chapter 7

# Regard Your Core Worth

*Think of what you have rather than of what you lack. Of the things you have, select the best and then reflect how eagerly you would have sought them if you did not have them.*

—Marcus Aurelius

The purpose of this chapter is to help you view your core worth accurately. People with little self-esteem tend to define their worth narrowly, conditional on some trait or behavior. As discussed, when they fail to demonstrate this trait or behavior then their self-esteem is threatened. By contrast, people with self-esteem feel secure in their worth. They realize that many desirable traits and behaviors *express* their worth, and serve as *reminders* of their worth. They do not let poor performance in an area define them. As they mature, they learn that humans express themselves in varied and complex ways, and they discover more and more ways by which they express their own core worth.

Patricia Linville (1987), a Yale psychologist, found that the more intricate, or complex, one's view of self is, the more resilient self-esteem is to stress. For example, the person who only sees oneself as a tennis player would be more likely to be deflated by losing a tennis game than a person who, with age and experience, has come to see oneself as a composite of many traits that are expressed through various roles.

Each person is like a seed of infinite worth, with every trait, in embryo, needed to flower. Those traits can be manifested in many different ways. For example, some express their creative talents artistically, some in the ways they problem-solve or survive, and others by the way they help people or show compassion. In some, the creative talents seem relatively—although never completely—dormant at present. Nevertheless, each person possesses some form of creativity in embryo. Likewise, each possesses some quantity of every desirable attribute in some level of development. Even a convict is honest *sometimes*. Even a gang leader can be quite creative in his communication or organizational skills (although with self-esteem, the gang leader might be more likely to use these skills for constructive, rather than destructive, purposes).

Each person may be compared to a portrait in various stages of completion. In one person, one area is quite developed and reflects the light in an interesting way. In another, no one area stands out above the rest, but several areas are somewhat developed, forming a unique and interesting pattern. We look at each portrait through the eyes of an artist, relishing the unique patterns and possibilities.

In the following activity you will more realistically and honestly recognize the value of your core self, and see that even now the core self is being expressed in ways that will remind you of your value.

## A Skill-Building Activity

This activity consists of three parts. Part I lists a number of personality traits that describe people. Part II allows you to explore traits that are especially important to you. Part III will help you realize how your responses uniquely demonstrate your core worth.

### *Part I: Personality Traits*

Rate yourself from 0 to 10 on each of the listed personality traits that follow. 0 means a complete and total absence of this trait (i.e., you never demonstrate it in the least degree). 10 means that this trait is completely developed, and that you demonstrate it as well as a human being possibly could. Try to be as fair and accurate as you can in your ratings. Do not inflate or deflate your ratings. Don't worry if you rate yourself higher on some items and lower on others. This is normal. This is not a competition against others. High ratings do not mean more worth. Remember that worth is already a given and is equal in all. We are just noticing unique ways in which worth is presently expressed. All of the benefit comes from being objective. Avoid all-or-nothing thinking and overgeneralizing.

Circle the appropriate rating:

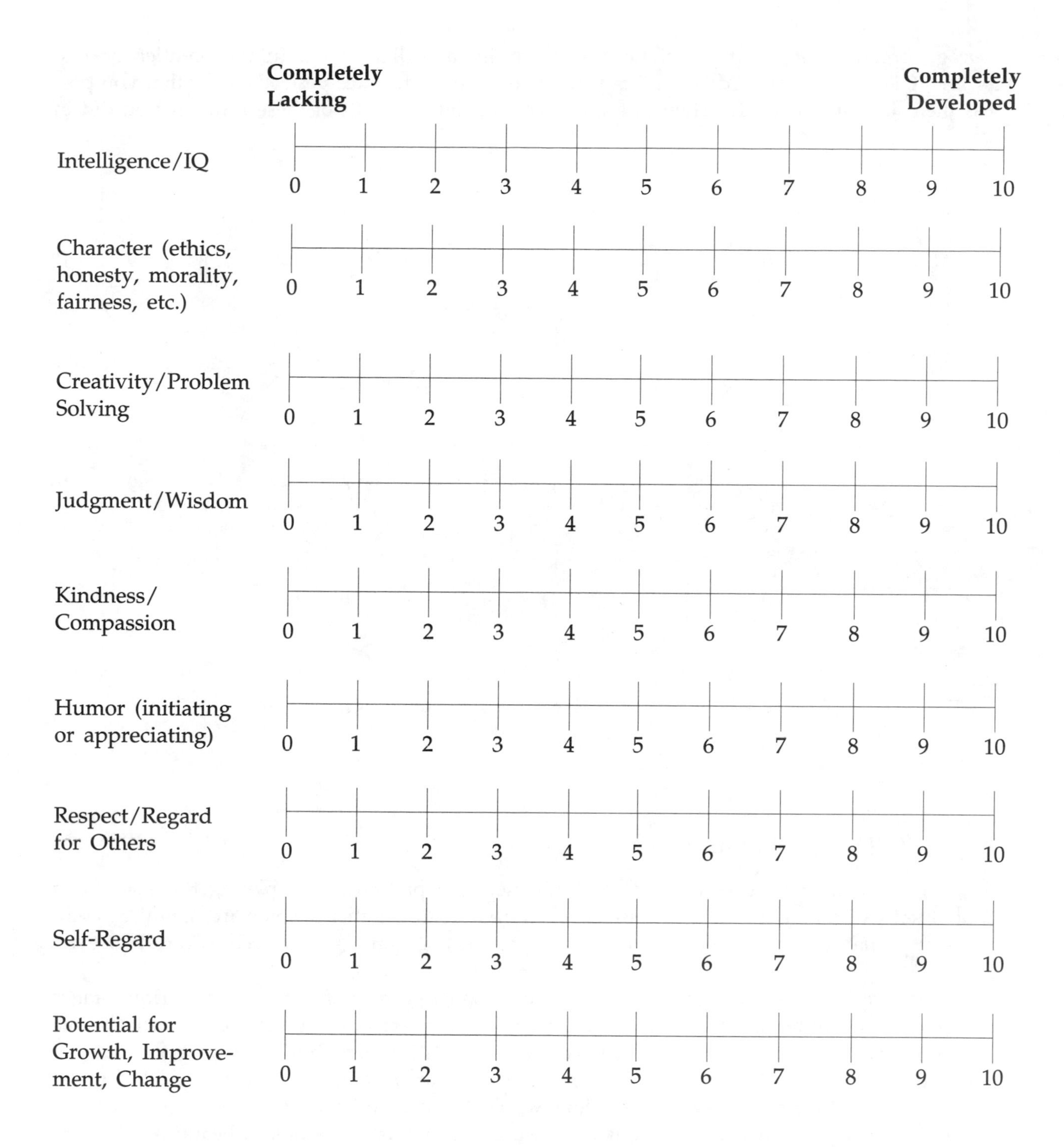


## *Part II: Additional Personality Traits*

In this part, list five additional traits that describe the way you contribute to the well-being of yourself and/or others. This will not be difficult if you consider the many attributes that describe human beings. Think of Benjamin Franklin's Thirteen Virtues (Tamarin 1969) (i.e., temperance, silence, order, resolution, frugality, industry, sincerity, justice, moderation, cleanliness, tranquility, chastity, and humility), the Boy Scout Law (A Scout is . . .), or other attributes you possess (e.g., appreciation, sensitivity, love, introspection, determination, orderliness, warmth, courage, organization, cheer, reverence for human life and dignity, playfulness, gentleness, discernment, etc.). The standard is not that you possess these attributes perfectly, only that you possess them in some measure. Then rate the degree of development of these traits as you did in Part I.

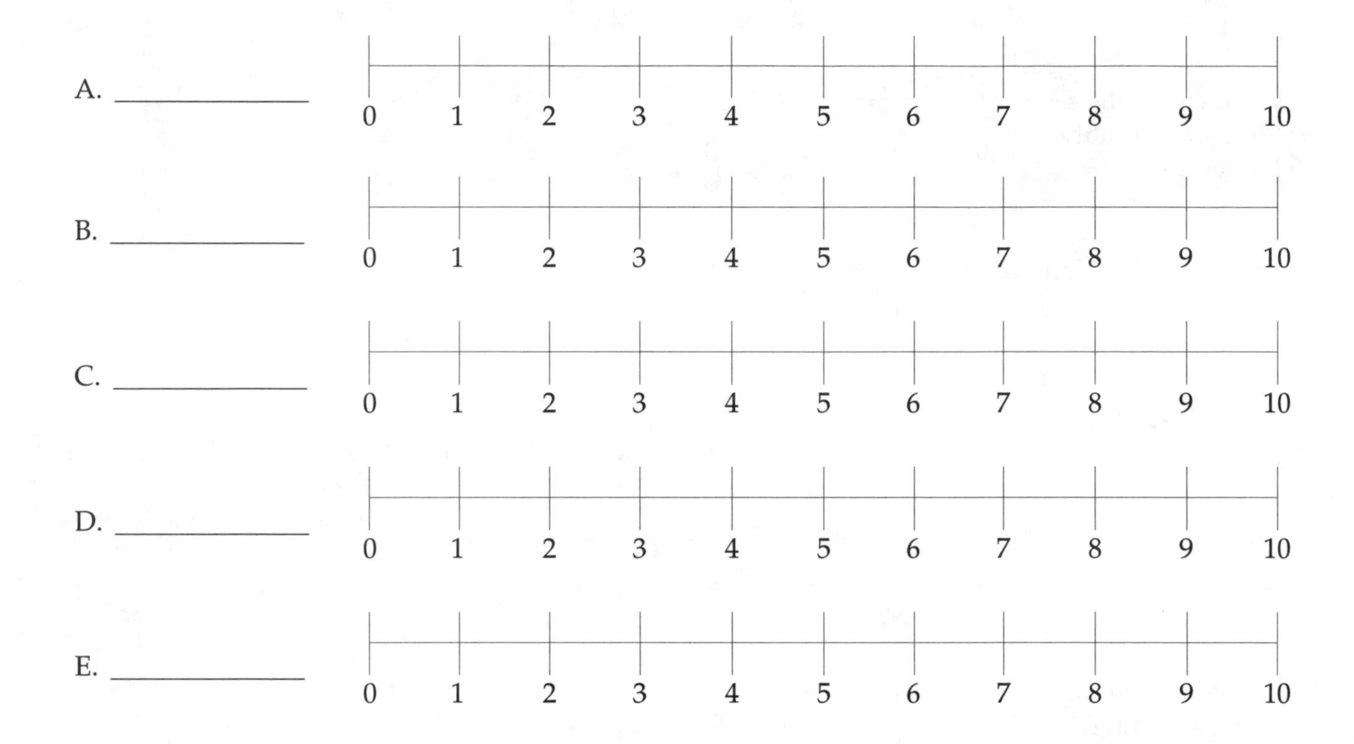


## *Part III: Interpretation*

Because humans are so complex and diverse, your pattern in completing this exercise is undoubtedly different from anyone else's. You were probably higher in some areas, lower in others. You probably also noticed an absence of zeros or tens, since such extremes rarely, if ever, exist.

This activity reveals a complex and unique personal portrait of attributes at various stages of development. Emerging from this composite is a more certain awareness of core worth. The idea of numerical ratings is not to invite comparisons with others, but to present an image of wholeness. It is much like a classic painting. Some colors are bright; some are dull. Each complements the other. Together, they form a unique whole. What about areas of low ratings? There are at least two ways to view these. One is to treasure yourself as you would a beautiful diamond with its inevitable flaws. Alternatively, you might view items of lower ratings as areas with the greatest potential for improvement, and savor the challenge.

Please respond to the following questions:

A. As you ponder your responses to Parts I and II, which attribute(s) do you feel best about?

B. The attribute(s) I give myself most credit for is (are) ______________________ because . . .

C. Let's consider the self-as-a-painting analogy. If an impartial observer were to consider the entire portrait, where would "the light shine brightest"? In other words, if a person were to take the time to see you as you really are at present, what areas would likely be most appreciated or enjoyed?

D. From this activity, I learned that . . .

# Chapter 8

# Create the Habit of Core-Affirming Thoughts

*Self-acceptance does not breed complacence. On the contrary, kindness, respect, encouragement, support, firm but caring discipline . . . these are the soil and climate for development.*

—Anonymous

People with and without self-esteem are fallible. They both make mistakes and fall short of goals and dreams. Both groups include people who are attractive, and some who are not. Both groups include people who have succeeded in business, school, sports, relationships, or other areas, and some who have not. What separates the two groups?

Research and clinical experience indicate that those with self-esteem think about and talk to themselves differently than those who dislike themselves. For example, upon failing, those without self-esteem (along with Type-A personality types and those high in test anxiety) have been shown to be very self-critical, thinking thoughts like: "What's wrong with me?"; "I should have known better!"; and "Why am I so dumb?" Such self-rejecting statements further degrade self-esteem. Conversely, those with self-esteem, Type-B personality types, and those low in test anxiety tend to appraise failures more compassionately, focusing on external factors and behaviors (e.g., "This test was hard"; "I had too many other demands on my time"; "I didn't study enough—I'll prepare better next time"). Such statements tend to preserve self-esteem in the face of stressful situations, enabling one to improve behavior without self-condemnation.

By focusing on what is "wrong" with themselves, people without self-esteem feel deficient and inadequate. They become defeated, losing motivation and the joy of experiencing oneself as worthwhile. If they do push themselves to grow, they do so with perfectionistic standards, in a driven and joyless fashion that paradoxically impairs success (Burns 1980). People with self-esteem, by contrast, acknowledge the rightness of the core, despite the rough edges and imperfections. By focusing on what is right, they motivate themselves to grow with a carrot, not a stick.

Cognitive therapy removes the negative thoughts that undermine self-esteem. This activity is practice in thinking the uplifting and self-affirming thoughts that build and preserve self-esteem.

## A Skill-Building Activity

Following is a list of statements representing the dialogue that people with self-esteem typically have with themselves. Focus on each separate statement, in turn, as follows:

1. Sit in a quiet place, well supported in a chair, where you will be comfortable for about twenty minutes.

2. Close your eyes. Take two deep breaths and relax your body as deeply and as completely as possible. Prepare yourself for, and expect, a pleasant experience.

3. Open your eyes long enough to read the first statement. Then close your eyes and *concentrate* on that statement. Repeat it to yourself three times slowly, allowing yourself to feel as though that statement were completely accurate. You might wish to imagine yourself in a situation actually thinking and believing that statement. Use all your senses to experience the situation.

4. Don't worry if a statement doesn't seem to apply to you yet. Just think of this as patient practice in creating a new mental habit. Don't allow negative or pessimistic thoughts to distract you or undermine your progress. Accept whatever actually happens, without demanding perfection. If a statement does not feel right, bypass it and return to it later. Or modify it so that it does feel right, keeping it positive though.

5. Repeat step three for each statement listed. The entire exercise will take about twenty minutes.

6. Repeat this activity each day for six days.

7. Each day, after doing this activity, notice how you feel. Many notice that with practice the thoughts begin to feel more and more comfortable, becoming as trusted friends. Thoughts that do not become comfortable within six days will likely become so when you return to them at program's end.

## *The Thoughts of Self-Esteem*

1. I think well of myself. This is good.

2. I accept myself because I realize that I am more than my foibles, mistakes, or any other externals.

3. Criticism is an external. I examine it for ways to improve, without concluding that the criticism makes me less worthwhile as a person.

4. I can criticize my own behavior without questioning my worth as a human being.

5. I notice and enjoy each sign of achievement or progress, no matter how insignificant it may seem to myself or others.

6. I enjoy the achievements and progress that others make, without concluding they are more valuable than I am as a person.

7. I am generally capable of living well, and of applying the time, effort, patience, training, and assistance needed to do so.

8. I expect others to like and respect me. If they don't, that's okay.

9. I can usually earn people's trust and affection through sincere and respectful treatment. If not, that's okay.

10. I generally show sound judgment in relationships and work.

11. I can influence others by my well-reasoned viewpoints, which I can present and defend effectively.

12. I like to help others enjoy themselves.

13. I enjoy new challenges and don't get upset when things don't go well right off the bat.

14. The work I do is generally good quality, and I expect to do many worthwhile things in the future.

15. I am aware of my strengths and respect them.

16. I can laugh at some of the ridiculous things I do sometimes.

17. I can make a difference in people's lives by what I contribute.

18. I enjoy making others feel happier and glad for time we shared.

19. I consider myself a worthwhile person.

20. I like being a one-of-a-kind portrait. I'm glad to be unique.

22. I like myself without comparison to others.

23. I feel stable and secure inside because I rightly regard my core worth.

## Chapter 9

# An Overview of Unconditional Human Worth

So far, we have explored some very important ideas and skills related to the first building block of self-esteem, Unconditional Human Worth. Because future ideas and skills will build on these pillars, it is important to pause and review what we have learned thus far.

## Three Important Ideas

1. Each person is of infinite, unchanging, and equal worth, which comes with birth.
2. The core self is separate from externals. Externals can cover up the core, or help it to shine, but the worth of the core is constant (i.e., infinite).
3. People express their worth in unique ways and patterns, but each person, at the core, is whole, possessing all necessary attributes in embryo.

## Four Learned Skills

1. Replace negative, core-attacking thoughts (i.e., distortions).
2. Use the *Even though . . . nevertheless* skill.
3. Regard your core worth.
4. Create the habit of core-affirming thoughts.

## General Review

It is helpful to reinforce the ideas and skills you learned in the previous chapters. Therefore, please take a few moments to complete the following statements. You might first wish to flip back through the preceding pages to review what you've done.

- The ideas that have had the most meaning to me are . . .

- The skills that I would most like to remember are . . .

I am always grateful for the way the universe provides clarifying moments and insights. The following, by American suffragette Elizabeth Cady Stanton, was posted at a bed and breakfast inn:

> I thought that the chief thing to be done in order to equal boys was to be learned and courageous. So I decided to study Greek and learn to manage a horse.

The proprietress of the B&B, a wonderful woman, skilled with horses, noticed me reading the posting and said, "Isn't that a wonderful quote?" I said, "Yes, I wrote it down. But it makes me somewhat uncomfortable." Said she, "Why? I love the way managing a horse gives me a sense of control."

Said I, "I agree. It's a good thing to be learned and courageous. But the underlying proposition is all wrong, that one must do something to be equal (i.e., of equal worth) with another. It is good to do these things because they are satisfying, but not to be equal to anybody else. We already are."

## Factor II

# Experiencing Unconditional Love

# Chapter 10

# The Basics of Unconditional Love

Earlier we posed the question: How does one build self-esteem in the absence of parental antecedents? So far, we have explored the first building block, or factor, called Unconditional Worth. This factor is based on the accurate recognition of core worth. As such, this factor relates to cognition, or the intellect.

Factor II, Unconditional Love, is a beautiful and extremely powerful building block that primarily concerns the emotions. Whereas Factor I primarily concerns the *realistic* part of the definition of self-esteem, Factor II primarily relates to the *appreciative* part of the definition. Let us now turn our attention to this factor.

Unlike Unconditional Worth, a cognition which one thinks about, love is something you experience. Although philosophers intellectualize about it, people recognize it when they see it. Did you ever know anyone who didn't?

When Mother Teresa ministered to people, it didn't matter if it was a dying man in Calcutta or a spastic child in Lebanon—something fascinating happened. At the moment when they looked into her eyes, and felt the great love coming through them, they then no longer looked away. They became calmer and their countenance softened. Did they think, "Hmmmm . . . let's see, is this agape, eros, or filial love?" No. They simply recognized love and responded to it.

They felt it, by the way she looked at them, spoke to them, and touched them (Petrie and Petrie 1986).

## Basic Principles

1. Each person has been created to love and be loved, as Mother Teresa observed (Petrie and Petrie 1986).
2. Each person needs affirming (i.e., love) to *feel* like somebody of worth. That is, everybody needs a source to affirm that they are loved, accepted, and worthwhile. As the psychologist Abraham Maslow (1968) said, "The need for love characterizes every human being that is born.... No psychological health is possible unless the essential core ... is ... accepted, loved and respected." Thus, love is important. If you have not received it from others, it is good to provide it yourself.

## What Is Love?

It helps to have a clear understanding of the nature of love, which is the second factor of self-esteem and an important building block. Love is:

1. A *feeling* that you *experience*. One recognizes it when one sees it.
2. An *attitude*. Love wants what's best for the loved one at each moment. (Please note: Love for others and love for self are not mutually exclusive. Ideally, the attitude of loving encircles both.)
3. A *decision* and a commitment that you make every day. Sometimes you "will it," even though this may be difficult at times.
4. A *skill* that is cultivated.

Some mistakenly assume that love—and related feelings like appreciation, acceptance, and affection—are only feelings that we either have or we don't. Although anyone can recognize and respond to love, loving is something that we learn to do.

Television's Mr. (Fred) Rogers demonstrates Unconditional Love daily as he tells children, "I like you just the way you are." He sings the following song (Rogers 1970). Notice the messages of separating worth from externals, and of liking the core:

It's you I like,

It's not the things you wear,

It's not the way you do your hair—

But it's you I like,

The way you are right now,

The way down deep inside you—

Not the things that hide you.

Mr. Rogers was a sickly child, confined during ragweed season to the only room in his house with an air conditioner. At eight years of age, Fred visited his grandfather's farm. He rejoiced as he scrambled along the stone walls of the farm. Afterwards, his grandfather told him, "Fred, you made this day special by being yourself. Remember, there's just one person in the world like you, and I like you just the way you are" (Sharapan 1992).

This story demonstrates that we each stand on the shoulders of those who have gone before us and that *loving unconditionally is learned.*

## Two Stories of Love

It is easier to recognize love than to define it. The following two stories depict love nicely.

### *Love Finds a Way*

When seventy-year-old Bernie Meyers of Wilmette, Illinois, died suddenly of cancer, his ten-year-old granddaughter Sarah Meyers didn't have a chance to say good-bye to him. For weeks Sarah said little about what she was feeling. But then one day she came home from a friend's birthday party with a bright-red helium balloon. "She went into the house," her mother recalls, "and came out carrying the balloon—and an envelope addressed to 'Grandpa Bernie, in Heaven Up High.'"

The envelope contained a letter in which Sarah told her grandfather that she loved him and hoped somehow he could hear her. Sarah printed her return address on the envelope, tied the envelope to the balloon and let it go. "The balloon seemed so fragile," her mother remembers. "I didn't think it would make it past the trees. But it did."

Two months passed. Then one day a letter arrived addressed to "Sarah Meyers Family" and bearing a York, Pennsylvania., postmark.

> Dear Sarah, Family & Friends: Your letter to Grandpa Bernie Meyers apparently reached its destination and was read by him. I understand they can't keep material things up there, so it drifted back to Earth. They just keep thoughts, memories, love, and things like that. Sarah, whenever you think about your grandpa, he knows and is very close by with overwhelming love. Sincerely, Don Kopp (also a grandpa).

Kopp, a sixty-three-year-old retired receiving clerk, had found the letter and the nearly deflated balloon while hunting in northeastern Pennsylvania—almost six hundred miles from Wilmette. The balloon had floated over at least three states and one of the Great Lakes before coming to rest on a blueberry bush.

"Though it took me a couple of days to think of what to say," Kopp notes, "it was important to me that I write to Sarah."

Says Sarah, "I just wanted to hear from Grandpa somehow. In a way, now I think I *have* heard from him."

—Bob Greene in the *Chicago Tribune* (1990)

### *Learning about Love: A Story about Mother Teresa*

My own mother used to be very busy the whole day, but as soon as evening came, she moved very fast to get ready to meet my father. At that time we didn't understand; we used to laugh; we used to tease her; but now I remember what a tremendous, delicate love she had for him. It didn't matter what happened that day; she was ready with a smile to meet him (Hunt 1987).

## Sources of Love

Love can be experienced from at least three sources, parents, self, and significant others. Theologians add an important fourth source, divine love. Most theologies teach that God's love is unconditional, a gift of grace, always accessible, and the securest foundation for growth. This spiritual foundation can be vitally useful, although a full exploration of God's love is beyond the scope of this book.

### *Parents*

Parents are an ideal source of Unconditional Love. Although it is nice if you received Unconditional Love from your folks, parents are fallible people who love imperfectly. No children ever received perfect Unconditional Love from their parents. It does no good to waste time begrudging the love that you did not receive in the past. As we discussed earlier in the book, blaming keeps you stuck in the past and contributes to your feeling like a helpless victim.

### *Self*

If one has not received love from others, one could ask, "How could I furnish the love I need to flourish?" One can provide this needed love in many ways, as we will soon see.

### *Significant Others*

The love of significant others, such as friends, spouses, or relatives, is intentionally listed as a last resource. It is nice to receive love from others; however, as with parents, others will never provide perfect Unconditional Love. The reaction we get from others is more likely to be a reflection of how they feel about themselves than a true reflection of our core worth. When people lack a realistic, appreciative opinion of themselves, they often become socially needy. That is, they turn to others for the approval of their core that they themselves lack and so desperately want. They can smother others and emotionally suck them dry. When their insecurity drives people away the rejection is devastating. Even if they win the esteem of others, this is *other*-esteem, not *self*-esteem. The esteem of others is no substitute for the inner security of self-esteem.

So the prudent course is to first be responsible for the source of love that you can depend on: That source is you. Before exploring ways to furnish wholesome love, let's explore some important additional premises regarding love.

## Additional Premises Regarding Love

Like worth, love must be unconditional, unshaken by temporary defeats, and independent of daily self-evaluations. In other words, one might say to oneself, "Even though I am performing poorly, I still love me."

Love also makes you *feel* like somebody. It doesn't define you or provide your worth. It just helps you realize, experience, and appreciate it. Perhaps you've heard the beautiful old melody sung by the Mills Brothers (1983), "You're Nobody Till Somebody Loves You." With no disrespect toward these wonderful performers, the song might better be entitled, "You're Always a Somebody, and Love Helps You *Know* It!"

Lastly, love is the foundation for growth. The reverse is rarely true. Hence, producing or overachieving usually does not fill the painful void of lack of love for the core self. Ted Turner, Gloria Steinhem, and astronaut Buzz Aldren are a few examples of people who succeeded brilliantly in producing and achieving, but realized later in life that something was missing *inside.* That something is a genuine feeling of affection for the core self. This affection is the soil and climate of human growth.

A number of authors have stated that people cannot love others if they do not love the self, and that even genuine, mature love from another cannot turn around self-dislike. Personally, I wonder if that is an overstatement. I think that genuine mature love from others can and does change one's self-concept. It is simply that one cannot always rely on the love of others. And if one is fortunate enough to find it, there is no *guarantee* that another's love alone will change self-dislike. So we return to the one area that a person can take full responsibility for, the self.

Dr. Joseph Michelotti's (1991) parents were immigrants from a small Italian farm who raised six children who became doctors, lawyers, and a physicist. They were raised with great love. His mother, especially, seemed to understand the value of the core self. Musing over her favorite portrait, she commented that when you died, "God gave you back your 'best self' . . . this is what I'm going to look like in heaven." She told Joseph, "You don't have to buy me a birthday present. Instead write me a letter about yourself. Tell me about your life. Is anything worrying you? Are you happy?" When in high school Joseph tried to discourage his parents from coming to watch him play in the orchestra for *The Music Man.* He reasoned that his role was unimportant. "Nonsense," she replied. "Of course we're coming, and we're coming because you're in the program." The whole family showed up. Great love, encouragement, and expectations for the betterment of mankind . . . a fine formula for building self-esteem. If you didn't receive these things from loved ones, then it is good to provide them for yourself.

## Reflections on Love

Before moving on to the next chapter, please consider the following reflections on love by Mother Teresa and actor Henry Winkler:

*Each individual person has been created to love and be loved.*

*There is a hunger greater than the hunger for bread . . . the hunger for love.*

*Small things with great love. It is not how much we do, but how much love we put in the doing. It is not how much we give, but how much love we put in the giving.*

—Mother Teresa

*A human being's first responsibility is to shake hands with himself.*

—Henry Winkler

# Chapter 11

# Find, Love, and Heal the Core Self

*If you didn't have loving parents, then you had better learn to be a loving parent to yourself.*

—Anonymous

Life is not about pedestals and power. Life is about love. As Mother Teresa said, each person has been created to love and be loved. It is love that really heals, not so much the intellect, although cognition supports the process.

In a sense, love is the foundation of effective stress management because it is the foundation of mental health and self-esteem. Stress management is really about managing life. It typically teaches skills to help one cope in the present, but largely ignores the power of healing the past so that we can enjoy the present. Recent studies (Pennebaker 1997; Borkovec, Wilkinson, Folensbee, et al. 1983) have shown that writing about one's past and present worries greatly improves the mood and the immune system.

There are various theories advanced to explain these results. Some think that putting pent-up worries or traumas on paper releases and discharges them, providing great relief. Some think that in writing about such concerns people gain distance, objectivity, perspective, and sometimes solutions. Personally, I think that there is another reason: Writing about feelings acknowledges and honors those feelings, which are typically disowned in shame-based people (i.e., people who feel bad to the core). Writing about your feelings is a way of loving yourself.

## Love Heals the Child within Us

There is within each of us a light . . . a core of peace, wholeness, joy, goodness, innate worth, and feelings/emotions that are good and that make us human. This core being is sometimes metaphorically called the "Inner Child." The Inner Child possesses, in embryo, every attribute it needs, plus the inborn tendency to grow and polish the rough edges.

With time, however, we usually—to one degree or another—separate or split from the Inner Child. We understand this process well: Abuse, abandonment, criticism, and/or neglect interact with personal fallibilities and choices. They lead people to conclude that they are defective and flawed as individuals. They don't believe that they *make* mistakes; but instead that they *are* a mistake, bad at the core. Thus, the core Inner Child becomes covered, rejected, disowned, split off, or separated. This is the root of self-dislike and shame-based behaviors that are common to so many stress-related dysfunctions.

The truth is, however, that the Inner Child—though battered, covered, and split off—survives intact. The child you once were, you still are (Leman and Carlson 1989). Our goal is healing, integration, wholeness, and reunion of our present consciousness with our inner core of light. The cure, quite simply, is love. We may not call it love in the helping professions, but it is love. Love heals and provides the foundation for growth. Although the adult operates logically, the core Inner Child hungers for love, and continues to cry out until that hunger is touched.

Adults understand this process well. In one of my stress classes we discuss parenting styles as they relate to stress. I'll ask if any of the students had perfect parents. After a little laughter, I'll ask if anyone had parents who were reasonably close to perfection. Among those who respond, there is usually a look of joy on their faces as they relate how feelings were expressed and respected, and how time and affection were freely given. Typically these students are doing well in school and life, and they are not neurotically driven individuals. By contrast, those whose need for love has not yet been touched are more likely to experience insecurity, joyless striving, social neediness, anger, and status concern.

## Corrective Experiences Repair Early Wounds

The question: Can the adult heal the "hole in the soul" if love was in short supply developmentally? The answer is yes. One approach comes from alcoholism and dysfunctional family literature. This approach uses imagery, which emphasizes affect coupled with reason. Since many people had imperfect pasts, corrective experiences can settle the past so we can move ahead (Alexander 1932). Below are the instructions for two corrective experiences, adapted from the works of John Bradshaw (1988) and Pam Levin (1988).

### *Corrective Experience No. 1: Find and Love the Core Self*

The purpose of this five-step exercise is to find and love your core self, or your Inner Child.

1. First, write down names of your most cherished friends, family members, and/or loved ones; people you feel/felt good to be with; people who make/made you feel warm, safe,

accepted, loved. First identify couples, then individuals (including friends, colleagues, teachers).

2. Find a place to sit quietly and comfortably where you won't be disturbed for about fifteen minutes.
3. Take two very deep breaths, saying the word "relax" as you breathe out.
4. Imagine yourself as an infant, surrounded by loving people. These can be the loving people you identified, or two warm, loving grown-ups, one a male and one a female. You can imagine parents, as you would have liked your parents to ideally be. Perhaps you imagine composite figures of people you have known and loved, who made you feel like a somebody—a person of worth.
5. As an infant you needed to hear the words that follow. Imagine yourself hearing the statements below alternately from a male voice and a female voice.

- We're so glad you're here.
- Welcome to the world.
- Welcome to our family and home.
- We're so glad you're a boy (or a girl).
- You're beautiful.
- All our children are beautiful.
- We want to be near you, to hold you, and to love you.
- Sometimes you'll feel joy and laughter, sometimes sadness and pain and anger and worry. These feelings are all okay with us.
- We'll be here for you.
- We'll give you all the time you need to get your needs met.
- It's okay to wander and separate and explore and experiment.
- We won't leave you.

Imagine the speakers of these words cradling you, loving you, gently gazing on you with eyes of love, as you respond to these feelings.

Practice this imagery for two consecutive days before continuing to the next corrective experience.

## *Corrective Experience No. 2: Embracing Your Lost Inner Child*

Again, find a place where you can reflect undisturbed for at least fifteen minutes. Relax and focus on your breathing for a few minutes. Being mindful of your breathing, be aware of the air as you breathe in and as you breathe out. Notice the difference in the air as you inhale and exhale. Focus on the difference. Now imagine the following, using masculine or feminine pronouns as appropriate:

> You are walking down a long flight of stairs. Walk down the stairs slowly and count down from ten to one. When you reach the bottom of the stairs, turn left and walk

down a long corridor with doors on your right and doors on your left. Each door has a colored symbol on it. As you look toward the end of the corridor there is a force field of light. Walk through the light and go back through time to a street where you lived before you were seven years old. Walk down that street to the house in which you lived. Look at the house. Notice the roof, the color of the house, and the windows and doors. See a small child come out the front door. How is the child dressed? What color are the child's shoes?

Walk over to the child. Tell her that you are from her future. Tell her that you know better than anyone what she has been through. Her suffering, her abandonment, her shame. Tell her that of all the people she will ever know, you are the only one she will never lose. Now ask her if she is willing to go home with you. If not, tell her you will visit her tomorrow. If she is willing to go with you, take her by the hand and start walking away. Feel the warmth and the joy of that tiny hand and of being with that little person. As you walk away, see your mom and dad come out on the porch. Wave good-bye to them. Look over your shoulder as you continue walking away and see your parents becoming smaller and smaller until they are completely gone.

Turn the corner and see your Higher Power and your most cherished friends waiting for you. Embrace all your friends and allow your Higher Power to come into your heart. See them all embracing the child with joy. Embrace your child and feel her warmly embrace you. Hold your child in your hand and let her shrink to the size of your hand. Or, embrace the child and feel her absorb into you, filling you with all her joy, hope, and potential. Tell her that you're placing her in your heart so you can always carry her with you. Promise her you'll meet her for five minutes each day. Pick an exact time. Commit to that time.

Next, imagine that you walk to some beautiful outdoor place. Stand in the middle of that place and reflect on the experience you just had. Get a sense of communion within yourself, with your Higher Power, and with all things. Now look up in the sky; see the purple white clouds form the number five. See the five become a four, be aware of your feet and legs. See the four become a three, feel the life in your stomach and in your arms. See the three become a two, feel the life in your hands, your face, and your whole body. Know that you are about to be fully awake—able to do all things with your fully awake mind. See the two become a one and be fully awake, remembering this experience.

Get an early photo of yourself, if you can, to remind you of the child that lives within you. Practice this imagery for two consecutive days.

I often ask students to locate and bring an early photo of themselves to class, which they usually do with exquisite pleasure. I remember one student, in particular, whom I was having a difficult time understanding and liking. He was silent and withdrawn, and looked down when spoken to. Then he brought in a photo. He was standing as a child beside his immigrant parents. He had the pure and innocent look that only a small and sensitive child can have. From that time on I felt a great affection for that student and saw him through different eyes, eyes that understood his inner self. The true, likable self usually shows through in the child, before externals cover the core. To see the core is to be reminded of the miracle that each person is.

ADULT CHILDREN OF NORMAL PARENTS,
ANNUAL CONVENTION.

## Chapter 12

# The Language of Love

Loving relationships that last are characterized by appreciation, liking, respect, and acceptance. In healthy relationships, there seems to be the unspoken thoughts, "You know, I realized a long time ago that you are not perfect, not exactly what I expected. I might laugh with you about some of your preferences and idiosyncrasies, but you know that underneath the humor is genuine liking. And I'll never speak with contempt or ridicule." This atmosphere of respect, paradoxically, allows people to change and grow, if they choose to. Similarly, an attitude of kindness toward oneself also encourages and sustains growth.

We have seen how a negative internal dialogue can sabotage growth and life enjoyment. The skills to follow reinforce the decision to think of ourselves realistically *and* kindly.

## Kind Descriptions

Do you think of yourself as competent? Does this question prompt you to think, "Well, competent means perfectly competent. I'm certainly not perfectly competent. So I guess, in truth, I must be incompetent?"

This example of black and white thinking explains why it is difficult for many people to think well of themselves. Diagrammed, the thought process looks like this:

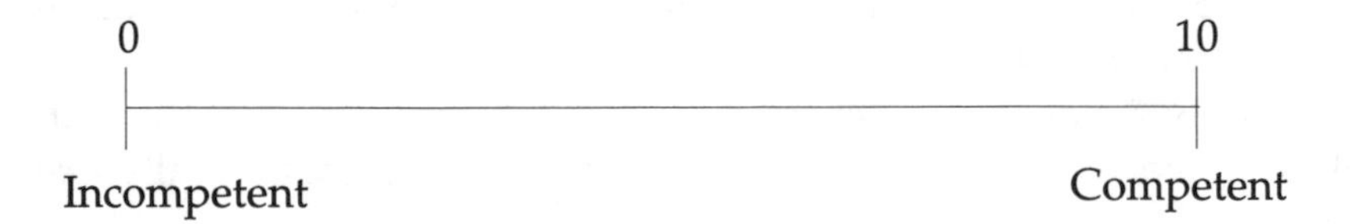


Here, competent suggests *perfect competence*, while incompetent means *without any ability; totally unfit*. By this line of thinking, if a person is not a 10, they must be a 0. In chapter six we suggested a way to rate behavior without rating the self. Here we suggest another way to think of the self that is accurate and kind. It looks like this:

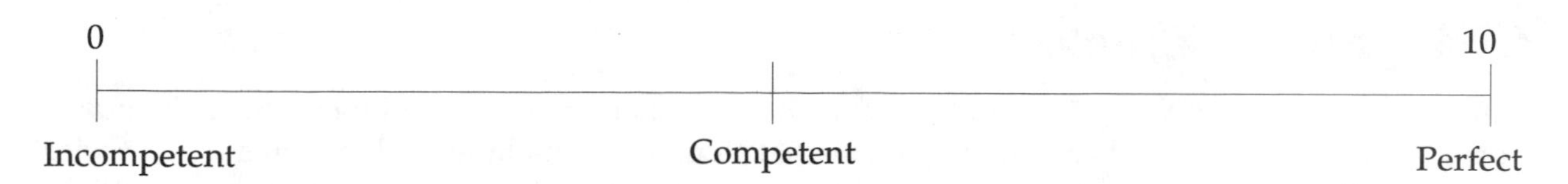


This way of thinking accurately acknowledges the middle ground. Of course, no one is perfect, which means completed and without flaw. Each person, however, is competent in the relative sense—competent at times and in unique ways, and possessing competence at some incomplete stage of development. By this standard, each person can be considered competent.

At the left end of the continuum below is a list of negative labels. At the polar opposite is perfection. In the middle, are kinder, more accurate descriptions of people.

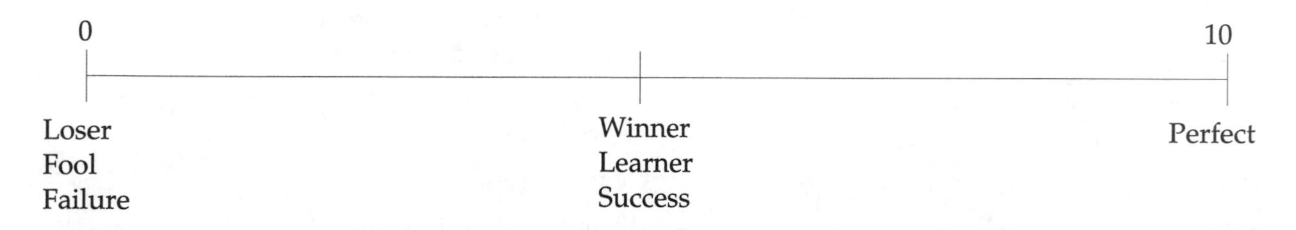


A *failure* is a person who is defeated without contributing or learning. Since anyone who is still alive is still learning and capable of contributing, then no one need conclude that they are a failure. If a *success* is one who learns, tries, and contributes at some level, then it is realistic for everyone to think of themselves as successful. This is not an argument for complacency. People can still aim for excellence and for doing their best, without demanding perfection.

As an exercise, add some additional labels to the list below. In the center, write a kinder, more accurate description than the word at the left.

0 — 10

Perfect

Idiot ______________________

Zero ______________________

Noncontributor ______________________

Unlikable ______________________

______________ ______________________

______________ ______________________

______________ ______________________

______________ ______________________

## Changing Channels

Below is listed some X-rated self-talk and comments that we make to others. Such language demeans and degrades. When you notice yourself thinking or making such comments, it is wise to immediately tell yourself "Stop!" and change channels. *Changing channels* simply means thinking and speaking about yourself respectfully—in ways that encourage growth and build self-esteem. Notice the emotional shift that occurs when you change channels.

| **X-Rated Self-Talk** | **Stop! Change Channels** |
| --- | --- |
| I'm only/just a _____________ (teacher, nurse, etc.). | I am a _____________ (teacher, nurse, etc.).<br>I am an honest, hard-working _____________.<br>I find satisfaction in being a _____________.<br>I am looking to advance. |
| I'll never succeed. | Success is exerting effort, and moving in the desired direction. |
| If only I'd _____________. | Next time I'll . . . |
| I hate this about me! | What an interesting quirk!<br>I'm going to work on this.<br>I'll feel even better about myself as I improve. |
| I'll probably blow this. | I'm not afraid to try, because my worth comes from within. |
| I am fat. | I have extra weight. I am working on this extra weight. |

### *X-Rated Self-Surveillance: An Exercise*

For the next two days, see if you can catch yourself making self-degrading comments. When you do, replace them with encouraging statements. Walking to class one day, I noticed a graduate student at a picnic table, deep in thought as she worked on this assignment. I quietly walked behind her and "snatched" her purse. As I walked away, I said loudly enough for her to hear, "Boy! That was easy. I hope there's lots of money in this purse." She laughed and turned red. She could have thought, "I am so out of it . . . I am such a space cadet." Later she showed me what she wrote. It said, "I concentrate well despite distractions like purse snatchers." A loving attitude truly is a decision that we make every day. When we choose a loving attitude, the desired feelings eventually follow.

| **X-Rated Self-Talk** | **Encouraging Comments/Thoughts** |
| --- | --- |
| First Day | |
| 1. | |
| 2. | |

Second Day

1.

2.

# Chapter 13

# The Good Opinion of Others

*We can make quiet but honest inventories of our strengths, since, in this connection, most of us are dishonest bookkeepers and need confirming "outside auditors."*

—Neal A. Maxwell

It is appropriate and may be useful at this juncture to summarize two key points about the love and approval of others.

1. The love and approval of others do not equal self-esteem. Otherwise, it would be called *other*-esteem, not self-esteem.
2. Love and approval of others, however, can aid the growth of self-esteem.

Just as criticism does not damage self-esteem without your consent, love and approval will not build self-esteem without your consent. This is not to discount the preciousness of intimacy; it's only to say that self-esteem is just that: *self*-esteem. If someone loves you and helps you to *feel* like a somebody, this is a wonderful gift for which you can be grateful; however, you can still have self-esteem in the absence of intimacy. For example, a widow living alone can have self-esteem.

Ask yourself, "What do I like about myself? What traits, attributes, skills, contributions, etc., do I appreciate?" Many, especially those with little self-esteem and those without practice, will find it difficult to answer these questions.

In the next chapter, you will make an honest inventory of your strengths. The exercise to follow can assist this process and serve as a warm-up. This exercise assumes that (1) you can assemble a small group of people who know you and each other reasonably well, and (2) group members are willing to anonymously share their favorable impressions of each other, in return for a very enjoyable experience. This exercise will take about an hour, depending on the number of people in the group.

## The Circle of Differing Gifts: An Exercise

Approval and affirming words from others do not equal self-esteem. However, allowing the good opinion of others in and examining them can help open our eyes to the truth. This can help stimulate a realistic, appreciative view of self that recognizes one's gifts.

1. Sit in a circle. Six to ten people is ideal, but any number can work. Each person has a pen/pencil and sheet of paper.

2. Each person writes his/her own name on the top of the sheet of paper in large letters.

3. On the signal "Pass," people pass the paper to the person sitting to their right.

4. The person who receives the paper proceeds to write three things that he/she appreciates about the person whose name appears on the paper. Entries could include qualities, strengths, attributes, contributions, etc. For example: I like your smile; I like the way you appreciate and draw my attention to the beauty of nature; I appreciate the way you express gratitude; You make me feel . . . ; etc.

   Scatter your comments around the paper so that no one knows who wrote the specific comments.

5. When everyone has completed writing three appreciation items, the signal "Ready, Pass" is given, whereupon each person passes the sheet to the person on the right. Each person then repeats the instructions for step 4.

6. Continue passing the papers until each person's sheet has been completed by the person on his/her left.

7. At this point, each person reads the comments about the person on his/her right. Be sure when you are the listener that you:

   - Relax.
   - Listen, enjoy, and allow each statement to sink in.
   - Give people credit for exercising good judgment regarding their comments about you.
   - Do not discount compliments with degrading self-talk (e.g., "Yes, but if they only knew"; "They're just being polite"; or "I sure snowed them"). If such comments arise, think, "Stop! What's happening here is healthy. I'll allow for the possibility that there is some or much truth to these comments."

The Circle of Differing Gifts is a wonderful exercise for people of all ages. It is a wonderful activity for families. Often, you'll hear comments like, "I never knew people thought such things." Good feelings among group members increase. Individuals enjoy keeping their own sheets of paper and referring to them when they need an emotional lift or a reminder of their strengths.

# Chapter 14

# Acknowledge and Accept Positive Qualities

Self-esteem can be cultivated by resolutely acknowledging what is presently "right" about one's self. For many, this is difficult because habits of negative thinking make it easier to identify what's wrong. Although there is a time and a benefit to acknowledging shortcomings and weaknesses, when this becomes the dominant focus—to the exclusion of strengths—self-esteem suffers.

This exercise, then, is practice in acknowledging and reinforcing strengths with appreciation. Doing this is a way of loving yourself. This skill is based on the research of three Canadians, Gauthier, Pellerin, and Renaud (1983), whose method enhanced the self-esteem of subjects in just a few weeks.

To warm up, place a check if you sometimes are, or have been, reasonably:

____ clean
____ handy
____ literate (come on—if you've read this far, check this)
____ punctual
____ assured or self-confident
____ enthusiastic, spirited
____ optimistic
____ humorous, mirthful, or amusing
____ friendly
____ gentle
____ loyal, committed
____ trustworthy
____ trusting, seeing the best in others
____ loving
____ strong, powerful, forceful
____ determined, resolute, firm
____ patient
____ rational, reasonable, logical
____ intuitive or trusting of own instincts
____ creative or imaginative
____ compassionate, kind, or caring
____ disciplined
____ persuasive
____ talented
____ cheerful
____ sensitive, or considerate
____ generous
____ appreciative
____ respectful, or polite
____ responsive to beauty or nature
____ principled, ethical
____ industrious
____ responsible, reliable
____ organized, orderly, or neat
____ sharing
____ encouraging, complimentary
____ attractive
____ well-groomed
____ physically fit
____ intelligent, perceptive
____ cooperative
____ forgiving, or able to look beyond mistakes or shortcomings
____ conciliatory
____ tranquil or serene
____ successful
____ open-minded
____ tactful
____ spontaneous
____ flexible or adaptable
____ energetic
____ expressive
____ affectionate
____ graceful, dignified
____ adventurous

Check the words that describe what you are sometimes reasonably good at:

____ socializer
____ listener
____ cook
____ athlete
____ cleaner
____ worker
____ friend
____ musician or singer
____ learner
____ leader or coach
____ organizer
____ decision maker
____ counselor
____ helper
____ "cheerleader," supporter
____ planner
____ follower
____ mistake corrector
____ smiler
____ debater
____ mediator
____ story teller
____ letter writer
____ thinker
____ requester
____ example
____ mate
____ taker of criticism
____ risk taker
____ enjoyer of hobbies
____ financial manager or budgeter
____ family member

Perfection was not required to check these items, since *nobody* does any of these all of the time or perfectly. However, if you checked a few of these and have managed to maintain reasonable sanity in a very complex world, give yourself a pat on the back. Remember, this was just a warm-up. The exercise that follows has been found to be very effective in building self-esteem.

## Cognitive Rehearsal: An Exercise

1. Develop a list of ten positive statements about yourself that are meaningful and realistic/true. You may develop the statements from the list on the preceding pages, generate your own statements, or do both. Examples might be: "I am a loyal, responsible member of my (family, team, club, etc.)"; "I am clean, orderly, etc."; "I am a concerned listener." If you mention a role that you perform well, try to add specific personal characteristics that explain why. For example, instead of saying that one is a good football player, one might add that he sizes up situations quickly and reacts decisively. Roles can change (e.g., after an injury or with age), but character and personality traits can be expressed across many different roles.

2. Write the ten positive statements in the space provided on the following page.

3. Find a place to relax, undisturbed, for fifteen to twenty minutes. For one or two minutes, meditate on one statement and the evidences for its accuracy. Repeat this for each statement.

4. Repeat this exercise every day for ten days. Each day, add an additional statement in the space provided.

5. Several times each day, look at an item on the list, and, for about two minutes, meditate on the evidences for its accuracy.

## Ten Positive Statements

1.

2.

3.

4.

5.

6.

7.

8.

9.

10.

## Additional Statements

1.

2.

3.

4.

5.

6.

7.

8.

9.

10.

If you prefer, you can write the statements on index cards and carry them with you. Some people find cards easier to refer to during the day.

Notice how you feel after practicing this skill, which disputes the all-or-nothing distortion "I am no good" by substituting appreciative thoughts and feelings. Students especially enjoy this exercise. Comments they have made over the years include:

- Hey! I am not so bad after all.
- I got better with practice. I didn't believe the statements at first. Then I found myself smiling on the way to school.
- I feel *motivated* to act on them.
- I felt peaceful and calm.
- I learned I have a lot more good than I give myself credit for.

# Chapter 15

# Cultivate Body Appreciation

The body is an external. It is not the core. One's body does not equal one's worth. However, the body is a metaphor for the core in that the way we experience the body is often similar to the way we experience our core selves.

The body, for example, is one way that we can receive and experience love. Consider the feeling of a hug or a gentle touch from someone who genuinely cares. The feeling that the body senses is also perceived by the inner core. If one views the body in the mirror with appreciation, it is easier to experience the core in a similar way. A respectful, caring attitude toward the body—reflected in sensible health practices—tends to positively influence one's feelings toward the core self.

Conversely, through mistreatment or ridicule the body can be shamed, and often, by extension, so is the core. If one thinks, "I would appreciate my body if I didn't have that blemish or that wrinkle or that fat," one would also be likely to place harsh conditions on loving the core self. If one is hard on one's physical imperfections, one will likely be unkind to the core self as well.

No matter how negatively one has come to view the body, however, or how negatively it has been treated, the inner core is still intact, responsive to healing, refreshing, restorative love.

As you cultivate appreciation for the body, it becomes easier to experience the core self more kindly. This exercise, then, will help you cultivate a wholesome appreciation for the body, no matter what its present condition. Although some in the world may have transmitted X-rated, critical messages about your body, everyone can learn or relearn to experience the body positively.

## The Magnificence of the Body

Following a distinguished career as a heart surgeon, Russell M. Nelson, M.D., (1988) has suggested: Consider the magnificent sights you have seen: a majestic mountain, a powerful horse gracefully galloping across a green meadow, a skyscraper. Now consider the magnificent body that you see in the mirror, ignoring any imperfections for the moment. The word *magnificent* derives from two Latin roots. *Magni* means "great"; *facere* means "to make." Thus, magnificent, or greatly made, well applies to the human body. Let us begin to appreciate some of the wonders in the treasure chest that is the body.

### *From Conception to Maturity*

At conception, a sperm and egg combine in a way that is only partially understood. From this union is formed a single cell that will multiply countless times according to a unique, unmatchable genetic code that is inherited—the sum of all of one's ancestors. The cells multiply according to this genetic code consisting of six billion steps of DNA. Though it could stretch the length of the adult's body, this genetic code is coiled within each cell's nucleus to a length of only 1/2500 inch. Soon after conception, cells are producing over 50,000 proteins needed for life. Although each cell contains the same genetic blueprint for the body, and could turn into any kind of cell in the body, cells specialize by activating and repressing certain genes. Thus, some cells become cells of the eye, others become heart cells, others become needed blood vessels or nerves that appear in their proper places at the proper times. Over the course of a lifetime, the cells of the body will manufacture five tons of protein. Each day the mature body produces three hundred billion cells, to maintain the body's total of seventy-five trillion cells. Placed end to end, the cells of the body would stretch 1,180,000 miles!

### *The Circulatory System*

The heart brings life to every cell. Weighing only eleven ounces, this magnificent muscle tirelessly pumps three thousand gallons of blood each day, beating 2.5 billion times over the course of a lifetime—a pace that would tire other muscles in minutes. The heart actually is two pumps side by side. One propels blood forcefully enough to circulate through the body's seventy-five thousand miles of blood vessels. The other sends blood to the lungs so gently that it does not damage the delicate air sacs there. When separated, cells of the heart beat with different rhythms. Together, however, they beat with the unison and synchrony of an exquisite symphony orchestra. Technology cannot replicate the heart's durability. The force of blood hurled against the aorta would quickly damage rigid metal pipes, while the flexible, tissue-thin valves of the heart are sturdier than any man-made materials.

## *The Amazing Skeletal System*

The 206 bones in the body are ounce for ounce stronger than solid steel or reinforced concrete. Unlike these man-made materials, they become denser and stronger with weight lifting. Sixty-eight constantly lubricated joints allow for incredible continual movement. For example, the thirty-three vertebrae of the spine, supported by four hundred muscles and one thousand ligaments, permit an infinite variety of head and body positions. Or consider the vast capacities of the hand—to powerfully turn the lid of a jar, or delicately remove a splinter. For durability, precision, and complexity, science cannot duplicate the thumb, whose rotation requires thousands of messages from the brain. The hand will tirelessly extend and flex the joints of the fingers—twenty-five million times over a lifetime. In incredibly efficient utilization of space, the marrow of the bones will manufacture 2.5 million red blood cells each second, replenishing a supply of twenty-five trillion red blood cells—which laid end to end would reach thirty-one thousand miles into the sky.

Ponder also the role of the body's 650 muscles. A simple step takes two hundred muscles: forty leg muscles lift the leg, while muscles in the back maintain balance, and abdominal muscles keep you from falling backward.

## *Sensing the World*

Sip a refreshing drink at a curbside cafe. You smell foods cooking and hear the sounds of people in animated conversation. You see multicolored flowers, people strolling, clouds lazily rolling, and feel the wind on your face. In less than a blink of an eye, complicated neural circuitry and countless signals in the brain allow you to sense the world around you. Let's consider the wonder of these capacities.

The eyes, ears, and nose are truly marvels of miniaturization. When you look at yourself in the mirror, you see in three dimensions though the image is entirely flat. Constant movement of the eyes, equivalent to walking fifty miles a day, and tens of millions of receptors in the retina that perform billions of calculations each second, make the eye more sensitive and priceless than any camera. Unlike the camera, the eyes are self-cleansing.

Conversation displaces the eardrum a distance equal to the diameter of a hydrogen atom. Yet the exquisitely sensitive ears enable us to distinguish individual voices and turn toward the source of the sound. In addition, the ears inform the brain of the slightest postural imbalance.

Compressed into an area smaller than a postage stamp, each nostril has ten million receptors for odors, enabling the brain to distinguish and remember up to ten thousand different scents.

Could you imagine a finer covering for the body than the skin? Under the average square centimeter (the size of the little finger's nail) are hundreds of nerve endings that detect touch, temperature, and pain. Not to mention one hundred sweat glands to cool and numerous melanocytes to protect from the sun's rays.

## *The Remarkable Defenses*

Each moment, the body defends against an army of potent invaders with a defense system that is more sophisticated than any nation's. The skin forms the first line of protection. Its salty, acidic makeup kills many, many microbes and keeps many other impurities from entering the body.

Each day we inhale seventeen thousand pints of air, the equivalent of a small roomful of air, containing twenty billion foreign particles. The nose, airways, and lungs constitute a remarkable, self-contained air-conditioning and humidifying system. Lysozyme in the nose and throat destroys most bacteria and viruses. Mucus traps particles in the airways, and millions of tiny hairs, called cilia, vigorously sweep mucus back to the throat for swallowing. Powerful acid in the stomach neutralizes potent microbes, which is why a child can drink water from a puddle and usually remain healthy. In the nose, incoming air is conditioned to a constant 75 to 80 percent humidity. On cold days, additional blood is sent to the nose to warm the air.

Those microbes that evade destruction trigger a most remarkable flurry of activity. Billions of white cells relentlessly ingest or slay invaders that have entered the body. Other cells of the immune system multiply and summon antibody-producing cells. (A million different antibodies can be produced, each specific to a single microbe.) When needed, white cells can trigger fever that helps to defeat invaders, and shut down fever when the battle is over. The lessons of the battle are preserved, as the immune system remembers the invader and the way to defend against it in the future.

Near the digestive tract, which absorbs needed nutrients, is the liver. In addition to five hundred other vital processes, this vital organ processes all nutrients absorbed by the intestines and neutralizes toxins. For example, in the eight seconds it takes for blood to flow through it, the liver greatly detoxifies caffeine or nicotine, which could be deadly if sent directly to the heart.

## *The Body's Wisdom*

Overseeing the myriad complexities of the body is the brain. Weighing but three pounds and containing one hundred billion nerve cells, this organ makes even the finest computer seem crude by comparison. Since each nerve cell can connect with thousands of others, each in turn connecting to thousands of others, the flexibility, complexity, and potential of the brain is truly awe inspiring.

The brain, for example, keeps the interior of the body remarkably constant to preserve life. If a person is living in the desert in 120-degree weather, the brain directs more blood to the skin to release heat and increases perspiration. In the Arctic, blood is diverted from the skin to critical internal organs, while shivering generates heat. If a person bleeds, water is pulled from tissue into the blood vessels and nonessential blood vessels constrict to keep blood pressure adequate. While maintaining internal equilibrium, the brain also makes decisions, solves problems, dreams, retrieves stored memories, recognizes faces, and affords unlimited capacity for wisdom and personality.

## *Other Wonders of the Body*

Consider how the body converts the "grain of wheat once waving in a field" to "the energy expended by the wave of our hand" (National Geographic Society 1986) or to living tissue—first by a complex series of transformations in the digestive tract, and then by even more complex transformations in the cells.

Appreciate for a moment the three hundred million alveoli, or air sacs, in the lungs, which exchange oxygen from the air we breathe for carbon dioxide from the body's cells. Spread flat, these alveoli would almost cover a tennis court.

Ponder the body's ability to repair itself. Unlike a table leg or a pipe, bones, blood vessels, skin, and other parts of the body can self-repair.

Many organs have a backup system: two eyes, two kidneys, two lungs. The single, vital liver, however, has an extraordinary capacity for regeneration. It will function if 80 percent is destroyed or cut away, and can rebuild itself in just a few months to its original size.

Contemplation of the complexities and magnificence of the body certainly helps us to regard our bodies with appreciation. Now let us turn to an exercise that also helps us experience our bodies with wholesome appreciation.

## Body Appreciation: An Exercise

Do you see that the way you view your body influences the way you feel about your core self? Dwelling on the negative is a cognitive distortion that keeps your focus on negative thoughts. As a result, your mood can become generally negative. In a similar way, you can keep your focus on the most negative parts of your body. You might look into the mirror and focus right in on the blemish or a less attractive feature. Similarly, you might focus on fatigue, illness, or a part of the body that is not working well. (This is not to imply that you should ignore fatigue, illness or pain. Rather, we're talking about the way you generally experience your body.) Soon, if you're not careful, the body is generally experienced negatively.

To increase your body appreciation, do the following exercise for a minimum of four days.

> At least six times throughout the day look at your body directly or in a mirror and notice with appreciation something that is *right* about it. Sometimes notice the jewels that were described above. Consider the miracles inside the body. Sometimes consider the skin, sensory organs, hands, fingers, or a feature that you consider attractive. Notice with appreciation what *is* working.

Chapter 16

# Reinforce and Strengthen Body Appreciation

The exercise that follows was created by a well-known teacher of self-esteem, Jack Canfield (1985), and is a very effective way to reinforce the habit of experiencing the body with appreciation. The exercise takes about thirty minutes. Read it slowly, or have someone read it to you slowly, in a quiet place where you will be undisturbed. Complete this exercise once each day for four days.

## A Mind Walk toward Body Appreciation

Welcome. Find a comfortable position, either sitting up in a chair or lying on your back on the floor or on a bed. Take a moment to get comfortable. And become aware of your body now . . . You may wish to stretch various parts of your body . . . your arms, your legs, your neck, or your back . . . just to heighten your awareness of your body. And now begin to take a few deeper, longer, and slower breaths . . . inhaling through your nose and exhaling through your mouth, if you are able to do that. And continue the long, slow rhythmic breathing . . .

Now, let's take a few moments to focus on and appreciate your body. Feel the air coming in and out of your lungs, bringing you life energy. Be aware that your lungs go on breathing, even when you are not aware of them . . . breathing in and out, all day long, all night long, even when you sleep . . . breathing in oxygen, breathing in fresh pure air, breathing out the waste products, cleansing and restoring the entire body, a constant inflow and outflow of air . . . just like the ocean, like the tide coming in and going out. And so just now, send a beautiful and radiant white light and love to your lungs and realize that ever since you took your first breath your lungs have been there for you. No matter what we do, they still keep breathing in and out, all day long. Now become aware of your diaphragm, that muscle below your lungs that goes up and down and continually allows your lungs to breathe . . . and send light and love to your diaphragm.

Now become aware of your heart. Feel it and appreciate it. Your heart is a living miracle. It keeps beating ceaselessly, never asking for anything, a tireless muscle that continues to constantly serve you . . . sending life-giving nutrients throughout your body to every cell. What a beautiful and powerful instrument! Day in and day out your heart has been beating. And so see your heart surrounded by white light and warmth, and say silently, "I love you and I appreciate you," to your heart.

Become aware now of your blood, which is pumped through your heart. It is the river of life for your body. Millions upon millions of blood cells . . . red corpuscles and white corpuscles . . . anticoagulants and antibodies . . . flowing through your bloodstream, fighting off disease, providing you with immunity and healing . . . bringing oxygen from your lungs to every cell in your body . . . all the way down to your toes and up into your hair. Feel that blood moving through your veins and arteries . . . and surround all of those veins and arteries with white light. See it dancing in the blood stream as if it were bringing joy and love to each cell.

And now become aware of your chest and your rib cage. You can feel it rising and falling with your breathing . . . your rib cage that protects all of the organs in your body . . . protects your heart and your lungs . . . keeping them safe. So let yourself send love and light to those bones that make up your rib cage. And then become aware of your stomach and your intestines and your kidneys and your liver. All of the organs of your body that bring in food and digest it and provide the nutrients for you body . . . balancing and purifying your blood . . . your kidneys and your bladder. See your whole body from your neck down to your waist surrounded and filled with white light.

Next become aware of your legs . . . your legs that allow you to walk and to run and to dance and to jump. They allow you to stand up in the world, to move forward and to run and to make yourself breathless with exhilaration. Allow yourself to appreciate your legs and to feel them surrounded with white light. And see all the muscles and bones in your legs filled with radiant white light . . . and say to your legs, "I love you, legs, and I appreciate all the work that you've done." And then become aware of your feet. They let you stay balanced as you go through the world. They allow you to climb and to run . . . and they support you every day . . . and so thank your feet for being there and supporting you.

And then become aware of your arms. Your arms are miracles, too. And your hands. Think of all the things you are able to do because of your hands and your arms. You can write and type . . . you can reach out and touch things. You can pick things up and use them. You can bring food to your mouth. You can put things away that you don't want. You can scratch and itch, turn the pages of a book, cook food, drive your car, give someone a massage, tickle someone, defend yourself, or give someone a hug. You can reach out and make contact with your world and with others. So see your arms and your hands surrounded with light, and send them your love.

And then allow yourself to feel gratitude for having a body, one that you can use every day, to have the experiences you want to have, and that you need to grow and to learn from.

Then become aware of your spine, which allows you to stand up straight . . . and provides a structure for your whole body . . . and provides protection for your nerves that go from your brain down your spine and out to the rest of your body. See a golden light floating up your spine, from the base of your spine at your pelvis . . . floating up your spine one vertebra at a time, moving up your spine, all the way up to your neck . . . to the top of your spine where your skull connects . . . and let that golden light flow up into your brain.

And become aware of your vocal cords in your neck . . . they allow you to speak, to be heard, to communicate, to be understood, and to sing and to chant and to pray, and to shout, and yell with delight and excitement . . . to express your feelings and to cry and to share your deepest thoughts and your dreams.

Then become aware of the left side of your brain, the part of your brain that analyzes and computes, that solves problems and plans for the future, that calculates and reasons and deducts and inducts . . . just allow yourself to appreciate what your intellect provides for you . . . and see the left side of your brain totally filled with golden and white light . . . and shimmering little stars, and see that white light cleanse and awaken and love and nurture that part of your brain . . . and then let that light begin to flow across the bridge from the left side of your brain to the right side of your brain . . . the part of your brain that allows you to feel, to have emotions, to be intuitive, to dream . . . to daydream and to visualize, to create, and to talk to your higher wisdom . . . the part of your brain that allows you to write poetry and to draw . . . and to appreciate art and music. See that side of your brain filled with white and golden light.

Then sense that light flowing down the nerves into your eyes . . . and see and feel your eyes filled with that light, and realize the beauty that your eyes allow you to perceive: the flowers and the sunsets and the beautiful people . . . all the things that you've been able to appreciate through your eyes.

And then become aware of your nose. It allows you to smell and to breathe and to taste . . . all the wonderful tastes and smells in your life . . . the beautiful fragrances of flowers and the essence of all the foods that you love to eat.

Now become aware of your ears . . . they allow you to hear music, to listen to the wind, the sound of the surf at the ocean, and the singing of birds . . . and to listen to the words "I love you". . . and to be in discussions and to listen to the ideas of another, to allow understanding to come forward.

And now feel every part of yourself from head to toe surrounded and filled with your own love and your own light . . . And now take a moment and allow yourself to apologize to your body for anything you may have done to it . . . for the times you weren't kind to it and for the times that you didn't care for it with love . . . the times that you didn't listen to it . . . for the times that you put too much food or alcohol or drugs into it . . . for the times you were too busy to eat, too busy to exercise . . . too busy for a massage or for a hot bath . . . and for all the times your body wanted to be hugged or touched and you held back.

And once again feel your body . . . and see yourself surrounded with light . . . And now let that light begin to expand out from your body . . . out into the world . . . expanding out, filling the space around you.

Now begin to bring that light slowly back into yourself, very slowly, back into your body, into yourself . . . and experience yourself here, now, full of light and full of love and appreciation for your body . . . And when you're ready, perhaps you begin to let yourself stretch and feel the awareness and aliveness back in your body. . . And when you're ready, you can slowly begin to sit up and readjust to being in the room and just let your eyes open, taking as much time as you need to make that transition.

## *Practice Increases Affect*

This exercise can be quite powerful, and its effectiveness often increases with practice. As one relaxes and practices, useful feelings and insights may arise. Although the feelings that are experienced are usually quite pleasant, this may not always be the case. For example, one student became tearful the first time she practiced this exercise, particularly when she tried to appreciate her legs. She had wanted, as a youth, to be a dancer, but her legs had been seriously burned in a fire. She realized that she still had anger about the accident and had hated her legs ever since the accident. She determined to release the anger and negative feelings toward her body, and the next time was able to enjoy this exercise greatly. So keep practicing, and expect the benefits to increase over time.

# Chapter 17

# Assert Self-Love and Appreciation

Let us return our attention directly to the core self, and remember the premise that Unconditional Love is necessary for mental health and for growth. *Unconditional* means that we choose to love even though there are imperfections that we would wish to be otherwise.

Let's take two people who are overweight. Jane thinks, "I am fat. I hate myself." Mary thinks, "I am really glad inside to be me. I'd feel better and enjoy life even more if I lost some of this fat." Notice the difference in emotional tones between Jane and Mary. Which one is more likely to adhere to an eating and exercise plan to lose weight? Which one is more likely to arrive at the desired weight without being emotionally distraught?

In chapter six, "Acknowledging Reality: 'Nevertheless!'" you learned the following key concepts:

1. Acknowledging unpleasant external conditions without condemning the core self.

2. People who dislike the self tend to use *Because . . . therefore* thoughts (e.g., Because I am fat, therefore I hate myself) that erode self-esteem.

3. The *Nevertheless* skill provides a realistic, upbeat, immediate response to unpleasant externals—a response that reinforces one's sense of worth by separating worth from externals.

In this chapter, we expand the *Nevertheless* skill by using this format:

*Even though* ______________________, *nevertheless* ______________________________.
(some external) (some statement of love/appreciation)

For example: *Even though* I am overweight, *nevertheless* I love me.
Other *Nevertheless* statements are:

- I sure love myself.
- Inside I am really glad to be me.
- Deep down, I really like and appreciate me.

Another variation is using the *It's true* __________________, *and* __________________ format. For example, *It's true* that I performed poorly today, *and* I love me. Perhaps you can think of other sentences you like.

## Even Though . . . Nevertheless

### *Partner Practice: An Exercise*

Select a partner. Ask your partner to say whatever negative statements come to mind, be they true or false, like:

- I hate you!
- You're a loser!
- You're such a slob!
- Why do you always screw up?

To each criticism, put your ego on the shelf, and respond with an *Even though . . . nevertheless* statement that expresses love/appreciation for the core self. Again, you'll probably want to use some of your cognitive therapy or language of love skills. For example, if someone labels you "a loser," you could respond, "Actually I am a success who sometimes loses. *Even though* I sometimes lose, *nevertheless* . . ." If someone asserts that you always screw up, you can think, "*Even though* I sometimes screw up, *nevertheless* . . ."

### *Self-Love and Appreciation: An Exercise*

1. For each of the next six days, select three events with the potential to erode self-esteem (e.g., you notice bags under your eyes when you look in the mirror; someone criticizes you or calls you a name; you perform poorly; you remember that someone you love doesn't love you).

2. In response to each event, select an *Even though . . . nevertheless* statement that expresses love/appreciation. Then describe on the following worksheet the event or situation, the statement used, and the effect on your feelings from selecting this statement and saying it to yourself. Keeping a written record reinforces the skill.

3. This exercise allows you to experience challenging events with unconditional love. Such love is experienced as a *feeling*; try to say each statement with emotion. You might raise your chin a bit and place a pleasant expression on your face.

Remember that love is a feeling. It is also an attitude that wishes wellness for oneself at each moment; and it is a decision that is made each day. This is the essence of commitment. Commitment is intentional.

| Date | Event/Situation | Statement Used | Effect |
|---|---|---|---|
| ______ 1. 2. 3. | | | |
| ______ 1. 2. 3. | | | |
| ______ 1. 2. 3. | | | |
| ______ 1. 2. 3. | | | |
| ______ 1. 2. 3. | | | |
| ______ 1. 2. 3. | | | |

## Chapter 18

# Eyes of Love Meditation

This exercise is a nice way to help you experience yourself joyfully and with appreciation.

First, find a quiet place to relax undisturbed, either lying or seated, for about ten minutes.

Once you have settled in, imagine that you are sitting in the presence of a very trusted and very loving being—a dear friend, a loving family member, God, or an imaginary being. This being sees you realistically and very lovingly. Imagine that you can see yourself through this being's eyes—the eyes of love. What is there to appreciate? Look thoroughly.

- Is there something pleasing or attractive physically?
- Notice all pleasing personality or character traits, such as intelligence, brightness, insightfulness, laughter, humor, integrity, peacefulness, good taste, or patience.
- Recognize all talents and skills.
- Note the appearance beyond pure physical attributes, such as the countenance, expression, or smile.

Behold yourself through the eyes of love and appreciation, and enjoy the experience for a few moments.

Now reassociate back into your own body. Feel all those feelings of love and appreciation from this loving being—and feel warm, happy, at ease, secure. Say to yourself silently, "I am lovable," and feel those feelings of love and appreciation growing inside of you.

Chapter 19

# Liking the Face in the Mirror

This is one of the most powerful exercises in this book. I am grateful to U.S. Army chaplain N. Alden Brown for teaching it.

## What Are You Worth?

Some people reply:

- I am worth $12.50 an hour. That's what my boss pays me.
- I am not worth anything. If you don't believe me, ask my dad/spouse/girlfriend, etc.
- I'm not worth anything except for the morale of the troops.

As we have discussed previously, we cannot put a finite value on the worth of an individual. Do we do it? Yes, if we reduce a person to salary, insurance policies, rank or position, talents, or what we can take from them. So let's repeat here the basic tenet: Each person is of infinite, unchanging, and equal worth.

Have you ever taken a long time to look into your own eyes and see the core self? You can learn to like yourself in this way. It might take some practice, but this skill could change the way you think about mirrors.

The way other people view you may be distorted by the way they see themselves; however, a mirror reflects images quite accurately. When you view yourself in a mirror, your attention might be drawn to your appearance: your clothes, your hair, blemishes, or other externals. In this exercise, however, you'll see yourself differently, perhaps differently than you ever have before.

## A Reflection of Self: An Exercise

1. During the next four days, seek out a mirror several times throughout the course of each day.
2. Look into your eyes in the mirror with the eyes of love. As you look, you might first notice that there is stress in and around the eyes. Look with real understanding and emotion. Try to understand what's behind the stress and let it subside. As you look deeply with love you will notice a change in your eyes and in your entire countenance.
3. Repeat this exercise often. You can use the car mirror or any other mirror.

Over time, this simple yet profound exercise allows a very wholesome and good feeling to take root and grow. As you look into your eyes and see the core self, appearances and externals come to assume their correct (i.e., secondary) importance. You might notice that you begin to look forward to and enjoy looking into the mirror instead of dreading it because your focus is now on what is of infinite worth, the core—which you see with love.

# Chapter 20

# An Overview of Unconditional Love

In this section, we have explored some very important ideas and skills related to the second building block of self-esteem, Unconditional Love. Because this factor is so important, let's review some of the key ideas and skills.

## Supportive Ideas

- Love for one's core self is a wholesome feeling. It is also the attitude of wanting what is best for oneself, and a decision that is made daily.
- Psychological health and growth depend on love for the core.
- Love is learned and acquired through practice.
- One is responsible for cultivating love for the core self. One can count on this love, even if one cannot count on love from others.

## Acquired Skills

- Find, Love, and Heal the Core Self
- Kind Descriptions and Changing Channels
- Circle of Differing Gifts
- Acknowledge and Accept Positive Qualities
- Cultivate Body Appreciation
- Reinforce and Strengthen Body Appreciation
- Utilize the *Even Though . . . Nevertheless* Skill
- Eyes of Love Meditation
- Liking the Face in the Mirror

To reinforce these important ideas and skills, please take a few moments to respond to the following questions. You might first wish to flip back through the preceding pages of this section to review what you've done.

1. The ideas about Factor II that have had the most meaning to me are:

2. The skills that I would most like to remember and use are:

3. What do you need more of regarding Factor II exercises? Are there certain skills that you would like to practice more? Set aside as long a period of time as you need and practice them.

# Factor III

# The Active Side of Love: Growing

# Chapter 21

# The Basics of Growing

*Every decision we make is a statement of how much we value ourselves.*

—U. S. Army chaplain N. Alden Brown

Self-esteem is as much a matter of the heart as it is of cognition. This is especially true for the third building block of self-esteem, growing. Other names for growing include:

- Love in Action
- Completing
- Coming to Flower
- The *Even More* Factor

The "*Even More* Factor" derives from my most beloved teacher. Tall and gangly, some would say that he was not particularly handsome. In fact, some would say he was not good looking at all. But he knew his mother loved him, and so everybody liked him. He acquired his first suit, a blue one, at nineteen years of age. And when he put on that blue suit with a clean white shirt and tie, thinking how he would teach and serve others, he said—and his face lit up as he related this—"I became *even more* handsome!"

Factor 3, Growing, is the calm feeling of being *even more* of what you are at the core. In other words, Growing is developing the traits that exist in embryo. You feel deeply and quietly glad to be who you are because you know that you are being the best person you can be—at the reasonable and steady pace that is uniquely suited to you.

In short, then, Growing means:

- Developing our capacities and potentialities
- Ascending, moving toward excellence
- Elevating humanity, both others and the self

We have likened the core self to a crystal of infinite, unchanging worth—with every needed attribute in embryo. Factor I, Human Worth, accurately sees this. Factor II, Love, strengthens and shines the core and provides the foundation for Factor III, Growth.

Growing, or completing, involves scrubbing off remaining dirt and lifting the core into the light where it may shine even more brightly.

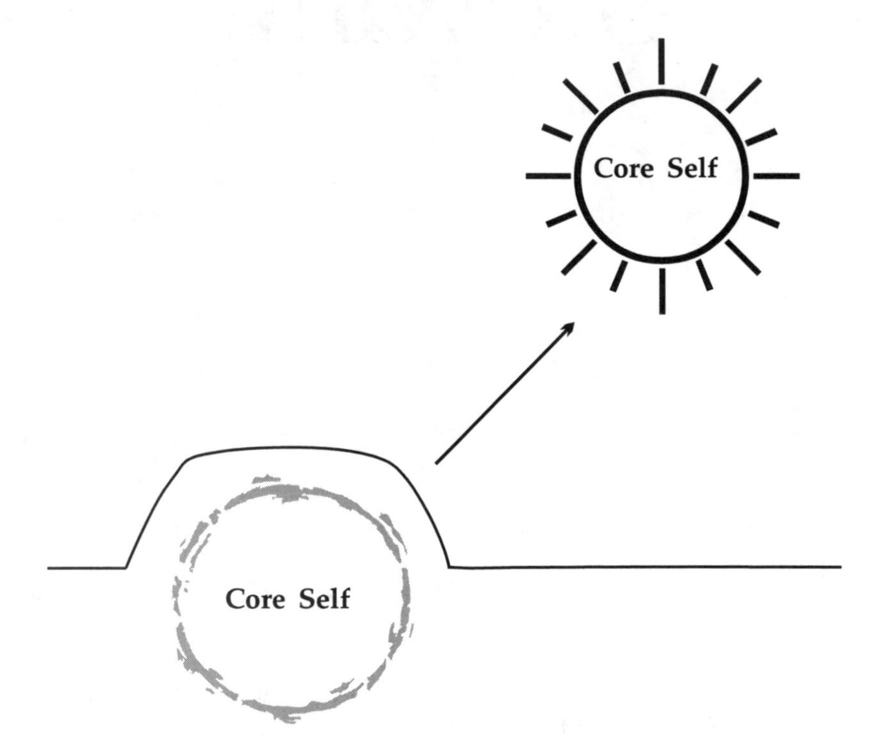


## Love in Action: The Next Steps

Having already removed the cognitive distortions that can camouflage or dirty the core, the next tasks are to:

- Choose behaviors that are loving and self-promoting.
- Remove from around the core behaviors that are not loving because they are not self-promoting. These include any practices that are unhealthy or unkind, including drug use,

excessive anger, sex that objectifies, etc. Unloving behavior also includes sleeping too little, eating too much food, inhaling too much nicotine, etc.

Personal growth is one of life's greatest pleasures. To repeat, self-esteem does not mean complacency. Hafen (1989) notes:

> [Some advance] the misleading idea that self-acceptance is the end of therapeutic or personal development rather than the beginning. Counseling can in this way become less concerned with assisting people toward change and more concerned with simply helping them to be more comfortable. That might be an adequate approach for helping someone come to terms with having a terminal illness; but it is unlikely to succeed as well in aiding the process of personal growth and development.

So self-esteem—the realistic, appreciative opinion of oneself—rests on the combination of self-acceptance (Factors I and II) and coming to flower (Factor III).

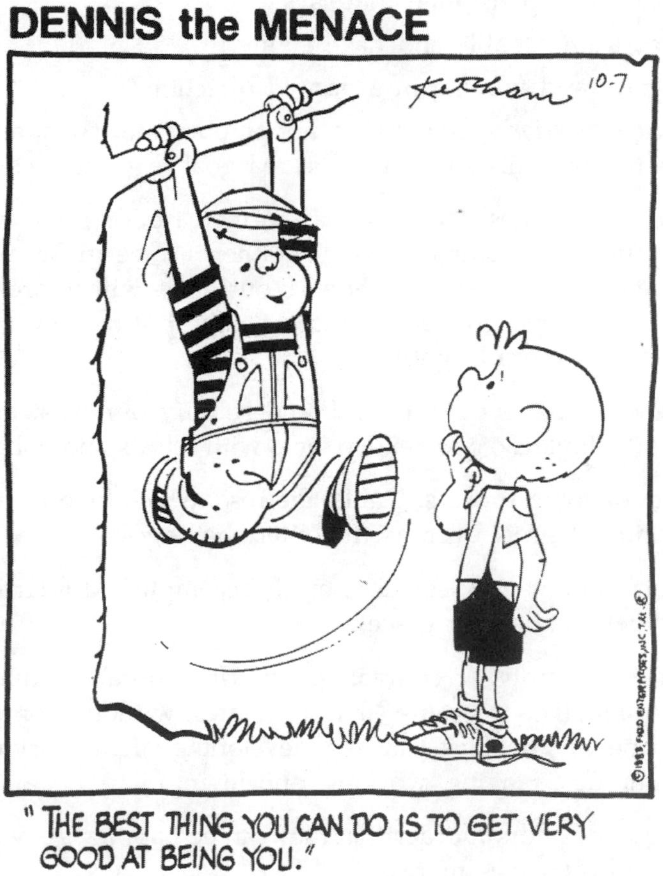
DENNIS the MENACE
Ketcham 10-7
"THE BEST THING YOU CAN DO IS TO GET VERY GOOD AT BEING YOU."

"DENNIS THE MENACE"® used by permission of Hank Ketcham and © by North American Syndicate.

## Perspectives on Growing

Factor III—the healthy growing process—rests on the following ten principles:

1. We are designed/created to develop physically, mentally, socially, emotionally, and spiritually—and will do so when our capacities are nourished and exercised. The nourishment is love.
2. Developing our capacities is a way of loving ourselves. Sharing them is a way of loving others.
3. Growing is an *outgrowth* of Unconditional Worth and Unconditional Love, not a *condition* for these. Love provides the soil for growth. In the absence of a sense of Unconditional Worth and Love, success/performance/producing rarely lead to self-esteem. Therefore, the decision to develop is best preceded by Factors I and II.
4. Growing does not mean a high degree of competence, since:
   - The research indicates that competence does not predict global self-esteem.
   - Competence, as it is usually used, implies an outcome (i.e., accomplished, finished, perfected).

   Rather, Growing is a perception that says:
   - "I can" (i.e., I am capable and have ability.)
   - "I am on track and moving in a desired direction."

   So Growing is a *direction* and a *process*, not an outcome. Thus, one can feel good about progress, even if one falls short of a desired goal (e.g., perfection).
5. Developing our capacities does not change, increase, or prove worth (worth exists at birth, already infinite and unchanging). Rather, as we grow: we express our worth; change our perceptions of self; experience ourselves with more joy, appreciation, and satisfaction; see our true, core selves more clearly; put ourselves in the sunlight where the core self shines more brightly.
6. Over time, good experiences with a friend solidify our trust and favorable opinions with that friend. Similarly, good experiences with self fix and enhance self-appreciation.
7. Growing is an ongoing process. Unlike the rose, which blooms and then dies, the core self can continue to grow even as the outer shell ages.
8. Growth is not completed in isolation, but is accomplished interdependently (e.g., with the help of others, nature, or grace).
9. Growing consists simply of cultivating *integrity* (moral conduct and character) and *wholesome pleasure* (i.e., pleasure that re-creates without compromising conscience, including: art, beauty, hobbies, learning, developing talents, serving, cleaning and beautifying surroundings, playing, working, and loving).
10. People choose to develop in order that they can be happier. As we are happier, we tend to enjoy life and ourselves more.

# Questions Regarding Growth

## *Are Integrity and Pleasure Somehow Incompatible?*

Integrity implies integration or wholeness. It implies that there is no division between one's behavior and one's values. When we develop integrity, we experience ourselves with more peace, and can say, with Winslow Homer, "All is lovely outside my house and inside my house and myself." Moral behavior becalms, and is kind, peaceable, and honest. Integrity is developed by starting the day with the decision, "Today I will put integrity first."

Although some have argued that pleasure is somehow incompatible with integrity, recall that the canonized Catholic saint, Francis of Assisi, said: "No man can live without delight, and that is why a man deprived of joy of spirit [i.e., joy of living, joie de vivre] goes over into carnal pleasures."

Gandhi further explained that it is not pleasure that corrupts the consciousness, but pleasure without conscience (e.g., pleasures that exploit, abuse, or violate trust). *Wholesome* pleasure is re-creative and necessary. Only the pleasures that degrade the human consciousness are to be avoided. In this sense, the pursuit of wholesome pleasure is consistent with the pursuit of integrity.

### *To Have Self-Esteem, Must I Have Perfect Integrity?*

Inner peace requires that one is doing the best that one knows how. One can do no more than one knows how and/or is capable. Since everyone is fallible, each person falls short of perfection. However, we can still experience our worth if we try our best to be on course and to be moving in the desired direction.

### *When Is Growing Not Fun?*

Growing is not fun when the outcome becomes a dire necessity. If, for example, one *must* develop into a successful salesperson as a condition of worth or happiness, then one will likely feel driven, not joyful. Again, we return to the fact that wholesome Growing assumes that Unconditional Worth and Love are first in place, so that one can enjoy the *process* of Growing without fear of failure or preoccupation with the outcome. Outcome preoccupation and fear of failure both derive from the same roots: *conditional* worth and *conditional* love.

Growing is climbing the staircase, not arriving. Thus, one can enjoy the progress and the direction without frustration for failing to arrive at perfection.

## Reflections on Elevating Humanity and the Self

Factor III is a pleasant, satisfying reaching—reaching beyond one's present level of development, and reaching out to others—as these reflections suggest. Please take the time now to ponder them.

*Once you have a self* [i.e., are secure in your own worth],
*then it is easier to lose yourself in selfless service.*

—Anonymous

*If I am not for myself, who will be for me? But if I am only for myself, what am I?*

—Hillel, *Wisdom of Our Fathers*

*I discovered that if I worked always and only*
*for all humanity, I would be optimally effective.*

—Buckminster Fuller

*The great failure of education is that it has made*
*people tribe-conscious rather than species-conscious.*

—Norman Cousins

*The great use of life is to spend it for something that will outlast it.*

—William James

*One knows from daily life that one exists for others . . .*
*A hundred times each day I remind myself.*

—Albert Einstein

*He could have added fortune to fame, but caring for neither,*
*he found happiness and honor in being helpful to the world.*

—Written as George Washington Carver's epitaph

*The desire to elevate humanity—the self, another person, all others—is what in everyday*
*language we call love. Love is wanting the very best for the object of our love.*

—John Burt

*If you have weaknesses, try to overcome them: If you fail, try again,*
*and if you then fail, keep trying, for God is merciful to his children,*
*a good deal kinder to us than we are to ourselves.*

—J. Golden Kimball

*If all else fails, try doing something nice for someone who doesn't expect it.*
*You'll be surprised how good you'll feel.*

—George Burns

*If you could follow this . . . rule* [your mild depression] *would be cured in fourteen*
*days. It is—to consider from time to time how you can give another person*
*pleasure . . . You would feel yourself to be useful and worthwhile.*

—Alfred Adler

*No man need fear death, he need fear only that he may die without having known his greatest power—the power of his free will to give his life for others.*

—Albert Schweitzer

[We are all] *craftsmen, investing our talents.*

—Laura Benet

*As we see what we can do we more fully appreciate who we are.*

—Anonymous

*Service is an eye toward others' lasting development.*

—Dallin H. Oaks

*The only way the magic* [i.e., growth] *works is by hard work. But hard work can be fun.*

—Jim Henson, Muppets Creator

*Some say principles are constraining. I say they are liberating.*
*Some say service is subservience. But I say it is ennobling.*

—Anonymous

# Chapter 22

# Accept That You Aren't Perfect

Growing is like climbing a mountain. If you know you have a firm footing, then you push up with confidence and it's fun. Factors I and II are the firm footings of growth. As you set out to grow and to enjoy the process, some people might "rain on your parade" by reminding you in one way or another that you and/or your efforts are less than perfect. The following *Nevertheless* skill varies slightly from the previous two *Nevertheless* skills in that it takes this form:

Even though *I am not perfect,* nevertheless ____________________.
(or some other statement of fact) (some statement of growing)

For example, someone tells you that you can't do anything right. You think:

Even though *I'm not perfect,* nevertheless *I'm growing.*

Other *Nevertheless* statements are:

- I'm sure trying.
- I'm learning.

- I'm on course and moving along.
- I'm still new at this and finding my way.
- I still enjoy trying.
- I think I can improve.
- My worth is infinite, I appreciate my efforts, and I have as much right to try as anybody.
- I still "work."
- I'm having fun.
- I'm developing in other ways.
- Learning is still adventurous.
- I'm more today than I was yesterday.
- I still persist/get it done.

Can you think of others that you like?

## Even Though I'm Not Perfect ... Nevertheless

### *Partner Practice: An Exercise*

Select a partner. Ask your partner to say whatever negative statements come to mind, be they true or false, like:

- My frog has a quicker wit than you do!
- Singing lessons? You?
- Your lousy memory lost us that account!
- You'll never amount to much!
- Why are you so slow?
- Your personality bugs me!

To each criticism, put your ego on the shelf, and respond with an *Even though I'm not perfect ... nevertheless* statement. Try to keep your sense of humor and respond with an upbeat feeling.

### *Accept Your Imperfections: An Exercise*

1. For each of the next six days, select three events with the potential to erode self-esteem.
2. In response to each event, select an *Even though I'm not perfect, nevertheless* statement. Then describe below the event or situation, the statement used, and the emotional effect you experience from selecting this statement and saying it to yourself. Keeping a written record reinforces the skill.

| Date | Event/Situation | Statement Used | Effect |
|---|---|---|---|
| ______ | | | |
| 1. | | | |
| 2. | | | |
| 3. | | | |
| ______ | | | |
| 1. | | | |
| 2. | | | |
| 3. | | | |
| ______ | | | |
| 1. | | | |
| 2. | | | |
| 3. | | | |
| ______ | | | |
| 1. | | | |
| 2. | | | |
| 3. | | | |
| ______ | | | |
| 1. | | | |
| 2. | | | |
| 3. | | | |
| ______ | | | |
| 1. | | | |
| 2. | | | |
| 3. | | | |

## Chapter 23

# Just for the Fun of It (Contemplating Possibilities)

Jim Henson, the creator of the Muppets, was appreciated widely for his childlike qualities, which refers to the enjoyable and precious qualities of a child. Consider the following childlike qualities:

- Sense of discovery/wonder/curiosity
- Vulnerable
- Warm
- Sympathetic
- Appreciative
- Enthusiastic

- Responsive
- Zestful
- Trusting
- Capacities to (Montegu 1988):
  - Learn
  - Live
  - Grow
  - Imagine/Fantasize/Dream
  - Experiment
  - Explore
  - Be open-minded
  - Love
  - Work
  - Play
  - Think

Although the storms of life might diminish the flames of some of these qualities, the ember of each quality is never entirely extinguished. A beauty of maturity is that one often has acquired the wisdom and emotional security to cultivate these qualities again.

## A Brief Inventory

Please record your responses to the following:

1 What do you like about your personality? (Recognizing strengths is a way of loving yourself.)

2. Answer the question "What would you like to change?" Use the following format:
It's true that I sometimes ____________________ so I'd like to be more ____________________
(describe behavior) (describe quality)

(There is no shame in having rough edges. However, notice the positive emotional tone of matter-of-factly acknowledging reality, while also noticing possibilities.)

# Attractive and Appealing Qualities

*Where there is no vision, the people perish.*

—Proverbs 29:18

What qualities of character increase a person's attraction and/or appeal? J. Brothers (1990), a contemporary psychologist, suggested the following traits as characteristics of older people who are experienced as attractive and appealing. One could argue that these characteristics apply to people of all ages, including you.

1. Put a check beside a trait if you agree that it would increase a person's attractiveness/appeal.

   ____ Cheerful

   ____ Poised

   ____ Aware

   ____ Delights in senses (enjoys food, nature, etc.)

   ____ Interested in the opposite sex

   ____ Enthusiastic about life

   ____ Upbeat (noncritical of others or self)

   ____ Healthy and vigorous (conditioned, hygienic)

   ____ Inner strength (learns from mistakes without agonizing over them)

   ____ Vulnerability (feels, allows own faults)

   ____ Relates with people as individuals (notices, smiles, talks to, thanks)

   ____ Kind

   ____ Good

   ____ Focuses on assets, not shortcomings

   ____ Fun (has fun, is fun, flirts sometimes for fun)

   ____ Expresses male and female sides; flexible

   ____ Enjoys friendships with both sexes (sees persons as whole, complex individuals)

2. Are there other traits you would add to the list? What are they?

3. If you were to select four traits to focus on—for yourself, just for the fun of it—which would they be?

   a.

   b.

   c.

   d.

## Chapter 24

# Take Stock of Your Character

Self-esteem is not positive thinking, where you tell yourself how wonderful and perfect you are, hoping that you will thereby become so. This kind of thinking is emotionally immature and stressful because it is not grounded in reality. People with self-esteem have no need to inflate themselves. Rather they are secure enough to accurately appraise both their strengths and weaknesses. Growth begins with an honest recognition of one's present level of development. The process can be quite self-affirming and optimistic when done with genuine regard for the core self.

This following activity is based on the Moral Inventory used in Alcoholics Anonymous. AA members teach that when a grocer inventories the shelves, he just counts what's there and what isn't. He does not judge; he just counts. When we inventory our own shelves, we simply count, without judging the core self.

This activity is called the Loving, Fearless, Searching, Honest Moral Inventory. It is *loving* because love casts out fear. With love, and without fear, we simply acknowledge where we presently stand. Fear results when a person negatively judges their core. What would be more frightening than concluding that one is bad to the core? The label "bad" is irrational because it implies that one is totally and always bad. The more realistic view is that one is infinitely worthwhile at the core, but possesses some rough edges. The inventory is *honest* and *moral* because we honestly search and identify both strengths and weaknesses. If we only found weaknesses, it would be called an *immoral* inventory. We consider something to be moral if it is in the long-term best interests of humankind, immoral if it is not.

The inventory will follow the BASIC MID pattern adapted from psychologist Arnold Lazarus' (1984) multimodal approach to helping. This approach assumes that people have strengths and weaknesses in eight dimensions of their lives, each dimension being represented by a letter in the acronym BASIC MID (Behavior, Affect, Sensations, Imagery, Cognitions, Moral, Interpersonal, Drugs/Biology). Seeing strengths and weaknesses side by side helps put our weaknesses in perspective. That is, we see weak areas as rough edges that can be strengthened and developed. They are not representative of the whole core. Related to each BASIC MID dimension are ways to grow and develop. Remember, acknowledging present reality can clarify your directions and goals.

## A List of Moral Strengths

*We can make quiet but honest inventories of our strengths, since, in this connection, most of us are dishonest bookkeepers and need confirming "outside auditors."*

—Neal A. Maxwell (1976)

Below are listed a number of qualities that could be considered moral strengths because they contribute to the best interests of humankind, including self.

1. Please check all qualities below if you, to a reasonable degree (i.e., not demanding perfection) demonstrate them:

____ integrity

____ compassion

____ love

____ virtue

____ knowledge

____ patience

____ kindness

____ humility/willingness to admit faults

____ respect for others

____ respect for self

____ honesty

____ helpfulness

____ supportiveness

____ affection

____ consideration/thoughtfulness

____ tolerance for diversity

____ trust

____ moral cleanliness

____ a sense of duty/responsibility

____ care for your reputation

____ forgiveness

____ friendliness

____ penitence/appropriate sorrow

____ hope/optimism

____ thriftiness

____ selflessness/service

____ sharing

____ gentleness

____ civility/courtesy

____ thankfulness

____ appreciation

____ dependability/keeping to your word

2. Circle an item above if developing it more fully would further your growth or happiness.

## Assessing Eight Areas of Living

On the BASIC MID Check-up and Planning Sheet you will assess your life in the following eight areas. Keep in mind, you are looking for general patterns. Certainly, most of us will at times experience many of the weaknesses mentioned.

1. **Behavior** includes things you do—acts, habits, gestures, or reactions. Strengths might include: punctuality, a pleasant expression, cleanliness, budgeting time for recreation, steadiness, measured speech, attractive dress/grooming, or accomplishing tasks at work. Weaknesses might include: avoiding or withdrawing from challenges, procrastinating, frowning or grimacing, defeated posture, being disorganized, controlling people, yelling, silent treatment, compulsive behaviors, and impatient or reckless driving behavior.
2. **Affect** refers to feelings you experience. Strengths could include optimism, peace, appreciation of self, contentment with what you have, cheerfulness, or calmness. Problems might include chronic depression, anxiety, anger, worry, fear, guilt, or self-dislike.
3. **Sensations** refer to the five senses. Strengths might include enjoying the wind/tastes/smells/sounds/sights. Problems/symptoms might be chronic headaches, tension, nausea, dizziness, stomach tightness, or seeing only negatives in the environment and not the beautiful.
4. **Imagery**. Strengths might be visualizing a pleasant future vacation, having pleasant dreams, or experiencing a pleasant feeling upon seeing one's reflection. Negatives might include nightmares, seeing oneself failing, a faulty self-image, or focusing on the negatives in the mirror.
5. **Cognitions**. Problems are indicated by the presence of distortions. Strengths are indicated by realistic optimism (i.e., everything won't be perfect, but I'll find something to enjoy, grow from, or improve) or cognitive skills, such as *Nevertheless* skills (see chapters 6, 17, and 22) or cognitive rehearsal (see chapter 14).
6. **Moral** refers to one's character and conduct. Strengths could include any of the qualities listed previously. Weaknesses would be the opposites.
7. **Interpersonal** describes the quality of relationships. Strengths would include good-quality intimate relationships, making family and friends a high priority, affiliating with people other than those you work with, and so on. Negative symptoms might include the absence of friends, aggression (e.g., name-calling, violence, or sarcasm), consistently withdrawing from people who disappoint you, or nonassertiveness (e.g., allowing oneself to be used).
8. **Drugs/Biology** refers to present health habits. Habits that reflect self-regard, and are therefore strengths, include adequate rest and relaxation, regular exercise, and proper

nutrition. Junk food, chronic use of tranquilizers or sleeping pills, smoking, or drug abuse generally reflects a disregard for one's health and/or oneself.

## *The Loving, Fearless, Searching, and Honest Moral Inventory*

1. Under each of the eight areas on the BASIC MID Check-up and Planning Sheet list present strengths, or what is presently going well in your life.

2. What are the present problem areas in your life? What do you notice that dissatisfies you? Describe these under Present Weaknesses for each of the BASIC MID areas.

3. As you review the present weak areas in your life, how would your life be different if you were to develop these areas? Describe your life in each of the eight areas. For example, if I were less anxious, what would I see or hear differently? How would relationships be different?

4. Under each of the BASIC MID areas, indicate what you could do to change/grow. Notice that the possibilities suggested are to reinforce strengths and to develop areas that are presently weaker. This can require your best creative thinking. For each weak area, there are many, many ways to develop, just as a weak muscle can be strengthened by a variety of exercises. For example, to improve health habits, one could read, join a health club, hire a nutritionist, or initiate a walking program with senior citizens. To reduce symptoms of anxiety, one could learn breathing control and muscle relaxation, or seek assistance from a skilled mental health professional. Excessive anger could be reduced by uprooting distortions, restoring self-esteem, applying healing skills, and/or learning to forgive. Many steps toward growth and development can be accomplished by yourself. Recognizing when help is needed and finding that help are signs of healthy self-esteem.

   Some interesting realizations arise in completing this exercise. For example, is alcoholism a moral problem? It is not if one views it as an addiction and refuses to judge the core of the addicted individual. It is if you consider that the *behavior* adversely affects the family of the individual and the person himself/herself. Do you, then, place alcoholism under the Drugs/Biology area or under the Moral area? In my view, this is not a critical issue. The purpose of the inventory is to help you increase awareness of areas that are affecting your life for good or bad. Because there can be overlap among the eight categories, it is not critical in which category a strength or weakness appears. What matters is only that they are acknowledged, and that you refuse to judge or condemn the core because you are imperfect.

   Take your time in completing the inventory. You might wish to sleep on it and return to it over a three-day period.

5. Select one entry from No. 4, one for which you feel reasonably confident about making progress and of finding enjoyment and satisfaction in the process. For a week, do what you need to in order to progress in this area.

6. Resolve to return to this planning sheet each month to see where you are in relation to No. 4 and to consider new goals.

Growth does not happen overnight. Some feel disappointed when it does not. Returning to the self-as-a-portrait analogy, it is helpful to think that a classic painting takes years to complete. In this case, however, the portrait is never finished; its evolution is an ongoing process.

## BASIC MID Check-Up and Planning Sheet

**(The Loving, Fearless, Searching, and Honest Moral Inventory)**

| Behavior | Affect | Sensations | Imagery | Cognitions | Moral (conduct & character) | Interpersonal | Drugs/Biology |
|---|---|---|---|---|---|---|---|
| **Present Strengths** | | | | | | | |
| | | | | | | | |
| **Present Weaknesses (Symptoms/Problems)** | | | | | | | |
| | | | | | | | |
| **How Would My Life Be Different If I Developed My Weaker Areas?** | | | | | | | |
| | | | | | | | |
| **What I Could Do to Change/Grow** | | | | | | | |
| | | | | | | | |

# Chapter 25

# Experience Pleasure

*The greatest challenge of life is how to enjoy it.*

—Nathaniel Branden

Between 1970 and 1990 the average American work year increased by more than 160 hours, and leisure time dropped in a corresponding fashion—despite improvements in technology. People tend to give up activities that give them pleasure when they're short on time (Lewinsohn, Munoz, Youngren, and Zeiss 1986). As a result of the stress and the absence of pleasure, their mood slips. The more depressed people become, the more their self-esteem erodes, and the less likely they are to believe that formerly enjoyable activities will bring them pleasure. So they fail to engage in the satisfying activities that would lift their mood and rebuild their self-esteem.

In the absence of leisure time, it becomes more difficult to define yourself apart from your job or paycheck. Harvard economist Juliet Schor (1991) reported that when workers at a British factory were forced to give up overtime because of hard times a physical and emotional recuperation took place. With time on their hands, including weekends and holidays, friendships developed and the meaning of life became clearer again. The idea of money lost some of its intensity. Even those with families to look after preferred the new arrangement, with very few exceptions.

So let's advance the proposition that finding pleasure in life is a skill that adults need to learn, relearn, and/or reinforce. The skill maintains emotional balance and improves self-esteem by helping us experience ourselves in a variety of pleasant ways. There is no suggestion here that one cannot, or should not, find pleasure in work; only that in the present culture there is a tendency for work to too narrowly define an individual. The activity that follows will help you discover, or rediscover, what is pleasant for you, and make a plan to do some of these things.

## Schedule Pleasant Activities

The following activity was developed by Peter Lewinsohn and his colleagues (1986).

1. The Pleasant Events Schedule that follows lists a wide range of activities. In Column 1, check those activities that you enjoyed in the past. Then rate from 1 to 10 how pleasant each checked item was. A score of 1 reflects little pleasure, and 10 reflects great pleasure. This rating goes in Column 1 also, beside each check mark. For example, if you moderately enjoyed being with happy people, but didn't enjoy being with friends/relatives, your first two items would look like this:

   _✓ (5)_ _____ 1. Being with happy people

   ______ _____ 2. Being with friends/relatives

### *Pleasant Events Schedule*

#### Social Interactions

These events occur with others. They tend to make us feel accepted, appreciated, liked, understood, etc. You might feel that an activity belongs in another group (to follow). The grouping is not important.

| Column 1 | Column 2 | |
|---|---|---|
| ________ | ________ | 1. Being with happy people |
| ________ | ________ | 2. Being with friends/relatives |
| ________ | ________ | 3. Thinking about people I like |
| ________ | ________ | 4. Planning an activity with people I care for |
| ________ | ________ | 5. Meeting someone new of the same sex |
| ________ | ________ | 6. Meeting someone new of the opposite sex |
| ________ | ________ | 7. Going to a club, restaurant, tavern, etc. |
| ________ | ________ | 8. Being at celebrations (birthdays, weddings, baptisms, parties, family get-togethers, etc.) |
| ________ | ________ | 9. Meeting a friend for lunch or a drink |

________ ________ 10. Talking openly and honestly (e.g., about your hopes, your fears, what interests you, what makes you laugh, what saddens you)

________ ________ 11. Expressing true affection (verbal or physical)

________ ________ 12. Showing interest in others

________ ________ 13. Noticing successes and strengths in family and friends

________ ________ 14. Dating, courting (this one is for married individuals, too)

________ ________ 15. Having a lively conversation

________ ________ 16. Inviting friends over

________ ________ 17. Stopping in to visit friends

________ ________ 18. Calling up someone I enjoy

________ ________ 19. Apologizing

________ ________ 20. Smiling at people

________ ________ 21. Calmly talking over problems with people I live with

________ ________ 22. Giving compliments, back pats, praise

________ ________ 23. Teasing/bantering

________ ________ 24. Amusing people or making them laugh

________ ________ 25. Playing with children

________ ________ 26. Other: ________________________________

## Activities That Make You Feel Capable, Loving, Useful, Strong, or Adequate

________ ________ 1. Starting a challenging job or doing it well

________ ________ 2. Learning something new (e.g., fixing leaks, new hobby, new language)

________ ________ 3. Helping someone (counseling, advising, listening)

________ ________ 4. Contributing to religious, charitable, or other groups

________ ________ 5. Driving skillfully

________ ________ 6. Expressing myself clearly (out loud or in writing)

________ ________ 7. Repairing something (sewing, fixing a car or bike, etc.)

________ ________ 8. Solving a problem or puzzle

**Column 1 Column 2**

__________ __________ 9. Exercising

__________ __________ 10. Thinking

__________ __________ 11. Going to a meeting (convention, business, civic)

__________ __________ 12. Visiting the ill, homebound, troubled

__________ __________ 13. Telling a child a story

__________ __________ 14. Writing a card, note, or letter

__________ __________ 15. Improving my appearance (seeking medical or dental help, improving my diet, going to a barber or beautician)

__________ __________ 16. Planning/budgeting time

__________ __________ 17. Discussing political issues

__________ __________ 18. Doing volunteer work, community service, etc.

__________ __________ 19. Planning a budget

__________ __________ 20. Protesting injustice, protecting someone, stopping fraud or abuse

__________ __________ 21. Being honest, moral, etc.

__________ __________ 22. Correcting mistakes

__________ __________ 23. Organizing a party

__________ __________ 24. Other: ________________________________________

## Intrinsically Pleasant Activities

__________ __________ 1. Laughing

__________ __________ 2. Relaxing, having peace and quiet

__________ __________ 3. Having a good meal

__________ __________ 4. A hobby (cooking, fishing, woodworking, photography, acting, gardening, collecting things)

__________ __________ 5. Listening to good music

__________ __________ 6. Seeing beautiful scenery

__________ __________ 7. Going to bed early, sleeping soundly, and awakening early

__________ __________ 8. Wearing attractive clothes

__________ __________ 9. Wearing comfortable clothes

________ ________ 10. Going to a concert, opera, ballet, or play

________ ________ 11. Playing sports (tennis, softball, racquetball, golf, horseshoes, Frisbee)

________ ________ 12. Taking trips or vacations

________ ________ 13. Shopping/buying something you like for yourself

________ ________ 14. Being outdoors (beach, country, mountains, kicking leaves, walking in the sand, floating in lakes)

________ ________ 15. Doing artwork (painting, sculpture, drawing)

________ ________ 16. Reading the Scriptures or other sacred works

________ ________ 17. Beautifying your home (redecorating, cleaning, yard work, etc.)

________ ________ 18. Going to a sports event

________ ________ 19. Reading (novels, poems, plays, newspapers, etc.)

________ ________ 20. Attending a lecture

________ ________ 21. Taking a drive

________ ________ 22. Sitting in the sun

________ ________ 23. Visiting a museum

________ ________ 24. Playing or singing music

________ ________ 25. Boating

________ ________ 26. Pleasing my family, friends, employer

________ ________ 27. Thinking about something good in the future

________ ________ 28. Watching TV

________ ________ 29. Camping, hunting

________ ________ 30. Grooming myself (bathing, combing hair, shaving)

________ ________ 31. Writing in my diary/journal

________ ________ 32. Taking a bike ride, hiking, or walking

________ ________ 33. Being with animals

________ ________ 34. Watching people

________ ________ 35. Taking a nap

________ ________ 36. Listening to nature sounds

________ ________ 37. Getting or giving a backrub

| Column 1 | Column 2 | |
|---|---|---|
| ________ | ________ | 38. Watching a storm, clouds, the sky |
| ________ | ________ | 39. Having spare time |
| ________ | ________ | 40. Daydreaming |
| ________ | ________ | 41. Feeling the presence of the Lord in my life; praying, worshipping |
| ________ | ________ | 42. Smelling a flower |
| ________ | ________ | 43. Talking about old times or special interests |
| ________ | ________ | 44. Going to auctions, garage sales, etc. |
| ________ | ________ | 45. Traveling |
| ________ | ________ | 46. Other: ________________________________ |

2. Next, place a check in column 2 if you've done the event in the last thirty days.
3. Circle the number of the events that you'd probably enjoy doing (on a good day).
4. Compare the first and second columns. Notice if there are many items you've enjoyed in the past that you currently are not doing very often.
5. Using the completed Pleasant Events Schedule for ideas, make a list of the twenty-five activities that you feel you'd enjoy doing most.
6. Make a plan to do more pleasant activities. Start with the simplest and the ones you are most likely to enjoy. Do as many pleasant events as you reasonably can. It is suggested that you do at least one each day, perhaps more on weekends. Write your plan on a calendar, and carry out this written plan for at least two weeks. Each time you do an activity, rate it on a 1 to 5 scale for pleasure (5 being highly enjoyable). This tests the stress-induced distortion that *nothing* is enjoyable. This rating may also help you later replace less enjoyable activities with others.

   Please note: If you are depressed, it is common to find that your old favorite activities are now the most difficult to enjoy, particularly if you tried them before when you were very low and failed to enjoy them. You might say, "I can't even enjoy my favorite activity," making you feel even more depressed. These events will become pleasant again as depression lifts. For now, start with other, simple activities. Gradually try your old favorites as your mood lifts.

## *Some Tips about Pleasure*

- Tune into the physical world. Pay less attention to your thoughts. Feel the wind, or the soap suds as you wash the car. See and hear.
- Before doing an event, set yourself up to enjoy it. Identify three things you will enjoy about it. Say, "I will enjoy (the sunshine, the breeze, talking with brother Bob, etc.)." Relax, and imagine yourself enjoying each aspect of the event as you repeat each statement.

- Ask yourself, "What will I do to make the activity enjoyable?"
- If you are concerned that you might not enjoy some activity that you'd like to try, break it up into steps. Think small, so you can be satisfied in reaching your goal. For example, start by only cleaning the house for ten minutes, then stop. Reward yourself with a "Good job!" pat on the back.
- Check your schedule for balance. Can you spread out the "need to's" to make room for some "want to's"?
- Time is limited, so use it wisely. You needn't do activities you don't like just because they're convenient.

## Little Things That Make Life Worth Living

By Mark Patinkin, newspaper columnist, *Providence Journal-Bulletin*

I recently wrote a column on little things that drive me nuts, like vanity plates, two-pound yippy dogs, and sticky floors in movie theaters. Afterward, a few less cynical types urged me to give equal time to the other side. So today, a second list:

- The smell of burning leaves in autumn.
- A hot shower when you're freezing.
- Pizza delivered to your door.
- Being the first in a crowded supermarket to notice a cashier announcing a newly opened register.
- Automatic icemakers.
- The one morning every six months that your three-year-old actually sleeps to 7:30 A.M.
- The service department saying, "No problem. That's on warranty."
- Hearing the phone ring just as you're sitting down to dinner, then realizing you have the answering machine on.
- Terrycloth bathrobes.
- That combined smell of ... new-mown grass ... and popcorn that hits you when you walk into a baseball stadium.
- Dogs that sense when you're sad and come over to make you feel better.
- Room service.
- Those two weeks in spring when even the drabbest shrubs are in full Technicolor.
- Having nothing scheduled Sunday morning except reading the newspaper.
- Learning at O'Hare Airport that your plane is at Gate 1 rather than 322.

- Heated pools.
- Cruising down the highway while the opposite lanes are in a five-mile traffic jam.
- The crack of a hardball against a wood bat.
- The zoo on a sunny day.
- A full moon just above the horizon at 7:30 P.M. when it looks the size of a dinner plate.
- A parking space four steps from the restaurant door.
- One-hour photo finishing.
- Deciding you've had it with the world, then checking your calendar and realizing you have nothing booked for the next five nights.
- Geese flying overhead shaped in a perfect "V."
- Lying on the grass in the countryside staring up at the brightest stars you've ever seen.
- Microwave popcorn.
- The airline ticket clerk explaining that they sold too many coach tickets and will be bumping you to first class.
- Eating a hot dog with a live baseball game in front of it.
- Blood-red autumn leaves.
- A cool breeze on a hot day.
- Your suitcase being the first one to appear on the airport baggage carousel.

If you enjoyed this reminder to appreciate life's loveliness, then you will probably enjoy also Barbara Ann Kipfer's *14,000 Things to Be Happy About* (1990).

# Chapter 26

# Prepare for Setbacks

You have now acquired a substantial number of skills to build self-esteem. Regardless of how secure one's self-esteem, there is still the possibility that it can be "blown away" by a salient "failure" or unfortunate event. So it is imperative to develop skill for riding out "failures"—for keeping self-esteem strong and secure during the storms of life that will inevitably come. In some ways, this activity is a review. Let's first preassess:

1. What are things at which people (including yourself) fail?

2. What does "failure" mean?

3. What has worked to help you cope with "failure" during, before, and after?

At what do people "fail"? Here are a few of the answers that adults have mentioned:

- jobs
- marriages
- parenting
- school
- reaching ideal weight
- smoking cessation
- keeping moral standards
- making time for fun
- reaching goals

Did you think of others?

What does "failure" mean? Some answers that adults have given include:

- Nobody loves you
- Rejection
- I'm no good
- Not maintaining my self-esteem
- I'm human

What has worked to help you cope with "failure" in the past? Some have mentioned talking it over, giving oneself permission to fail, forgiving oneself, realizing that it won't matter too much years from now, and changing course.

Are you getting the idea that people vary greatly in how they view failure and in their abilities to cope with it?

## Approaching Perfection

Let's take a look at "failure" in a way that expands some of the concepts previously explored.

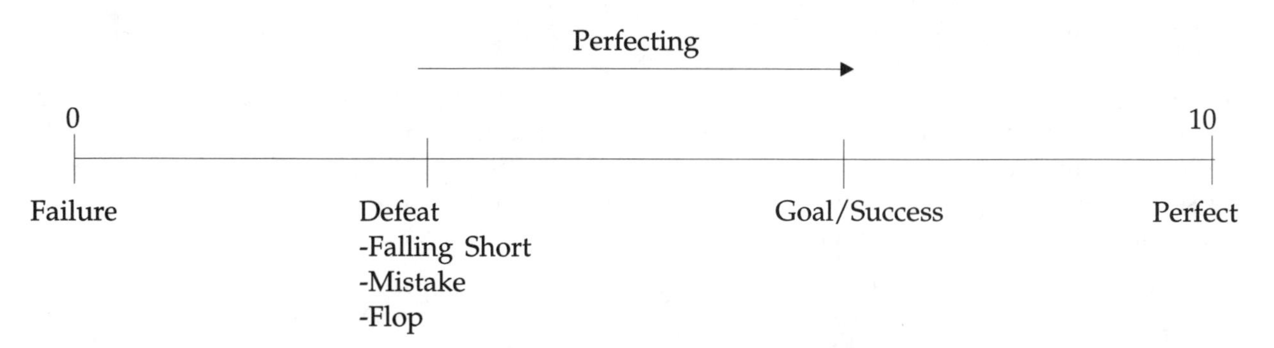


*Perfection* means completed, finished, without defect or flaw. Since humans are fallible, we only can approach perfection. A *goal/success* refers to attaining something we want for happiness, comfort, or growth. Because humans are always in the process of becoming, a goal is placed somewhat to the left of perfection. You might argue that you could set a goal to save 5 percent of your income and meet that goal perfectly. But aside from simply quantifiable endeavors, goals are generally imperfectly met. That is, improvements could ideally be made no matter how well one performs. *Perfecting* means making more nearly perfect. This can occur as one attempts to reach a goal or after meeting a goal.

People imprecisely say, "I'm a failure" (which means "I always and in every way fail"), when they mean to say, "I failed to reach my goal; I fell short of my goal; I made a mistake, etc." To slightly alter Hubert H. Humphrey's quotation to improve our understanding, "There's a big difference between failure and defeat. Failure is when you are defeated and [never] learn nor contribute anything."

## Handling Flops

Rather than using the label failure, I prefer the word "flop" to refer to unfortunate events/behaviors, falling short, mistakes, etc. Flop sounds less serious and less permanent than failure, and it refers to an external, not the core.

One more concept is worth reiterating before moving to the skill-building activity. Research demonstrated that a pessimistic thinking style held by men in their twenties predicted poor physical health when those men reached their forties and fifties (Peterson, Seligman, and Vaillant 1988). When an unfortunate event occurred, the pessimistic men tended to fully fault themselves, believe that they would never improve, and believe that misfortune would spill over into all areas of life. For example, after failing a math test, a pessimist would think, "It's me—I'm a failure; I always mess math tests up; I just am unlucky when things really matter." Optimists, on the other hand, who fared better years later in their physical health, might think, "I wasn't up to par physically that day; it's a one-time thing; this won't ruin my life." Similar thinking styles tend to distinguish drug addicts who relapse after slipping from those who rebound from similar setbacks.

From such research, we can form certain guidelines for handling setbacks:

1. Admit mistakes. Don't deny responsibility, but focus on remedial action: what you need to *do*.
2. Reframe the event. Instead of condemning the self, which erodes self-esteem and saps motivation, focus on externals. For example, instead of thinking, "What's wrong with me?" (The answer is easy: We're imperfect!), focus on externals (fatigue, incomplete preparation, too little experience, etc.).

Instead of considering something a total failure, remind yourself that there will probably be other opportunities. After experiencing a "flop," ask yourself the following questions:

- Did certain things go well?
- What are the advantages of not getting what I wanted?
- What coping skills could I learn from this?
- Were there signs of an impending crisis that I did not heed?
- If a similar event occurs again, what could I do to attend to such signs earlier?

### *Flop Inoculation: An Exercise*

Guidelines, such as those above, can be helpful. Let's put them into practice now. The following exercise derives from Stress Inoculation, developed by psychologist Donald Meichenbaum (1985). He states that people can prepare for stress by practicing what they will think and do before, during, and after encountering a stressful event. Exposure to small and safe doses of imaginary stress can "inoculate" us just as a small injection can inoculate us against disease. Here, the stressful event is the prospect of "flopping" (e.g., falling short of a goal, making a mistake, performing poorly, or forgetting to use your self-esteem skills when criticized).

### Step One

Put a check by any statements that would have meaning for you if chosen as part of your coping repertoire relative to mistakes/setbacks.

**Before**

__________ It will be fun to succeed, but not the end of the world if I don't.

__________ I'm new at this, so I'll be a little extra careful until I get the hang of it.

__________ I see this as a new challenge, not a problem or threat.

__________ This is a gift (opportunity, adventure, or challenge), not a problem. (Mother Teresa)

__________ I'll approach this with curiosity, not fear or self-doubt.

__________ I'll aim to do a good job. I won't ruin the experience with perfectionism.

__________ I have as much right as anyone to try my hand at this.

__________ I'll look for success in little steps and ways. I'll dismiss all-or-nothing demands of myself.

__________ I am embarking without absolute certainty of all the facts and outcomes, and that's okay.

__________ I have the right to decide what's best for me and to implement my decisions with confidence and without apology.

__________ I calmly examine the probable outcomes of my actions.

__________ If I'm not uptight about mistakes, I'll also be more creative.

__________ My focus is development, not mistakes.

__________ It's okay to try and to "flop."

__________ I'll choose the course that seems best.

__________ I'll relax and consider different approaches and their probable consequences ... Then I'll make the best choice I can.

__________ I'm optimistic and open to all possibilities.

__________ What will this challenge require of me? What can I realistically give?

__________ I don't have to be perfect to do well.

__________ It could be fun to try and stretch in the process.

__________ I'm not afraid to risk and fall short because my worth comes from within.

__________ What's the worst that could happen?

**During**

__________ This is difficult. Relax and focus on the task.

__________ Take it step by step. Feel good about little successes.

__________ It's too bad things aren't perfect, but they're not a catastrophe.

__________ Everyone makes mistakes and has rough edges. Why should I assume I don't?

__________ My quest to transcend and shape these imperfections is important.

__________ Relax and enjoy the process, glitches and all.

__________ I'm not Deity. I'm human. It's okay to be imperfect. I'll do my best.

__________ I focus on the process. The outcome will take care of itself.

__________ I'll take it one step at a time.

__________ Remember humor. It reminds me I'm neither as great as I wish I were, nor as bad as a lot of people might think.

__________ This informs me about my present limitations.

**After**

__________ I had a weakness. That was then. This is now.

__________ I'm just a beginner at this, and beginners have to expect mistakes now and then.

__________ This isn't a signpost to the rest of my life.

__________ I am hopeful.

__________ I take responsibility for understanding the situation, but not necessarily taking the blame, and never condemning myself.

__________ My judgment and behavior were bad, but *I* am not bad.

__________ Okay, now what? What are my options now?

__________ This revealed a weakness. This is part of me, not all of me.

__________ The weak parts are rough edges. At the core I am worthwhile.

__________ I love myself for this.

__________ I am still here for myself, to be a friend through this period.

__________ I have the courage to love myself when I'm imperfect (this is my foundation for growth).

__________ No matter what happened, I am still worthwhile, precious, and unique.

__________ I admit sometimes I'm this way. It disappoints me. I can do something about this.

__________ I accept the way I sometimes am, and I love those imperfect parts of me, too. This love gives me the security to grow in those areas.

__________ No matter how bad it seemed, certain things went okay. I've gained wisdom and experience.

__________ I'll change my course so I can be happier.

__________ I am teachable. I can change and grow.

__________ I can shape my future.

__________ I can use experiences from the past and convert them to strengths.

__________ I have the right to improve and develop each day.

__________ I have the right to make mistakes. I am adequate to admit them and repair them as much as humanly possible.

__________ This will pass.

__________ This will help me be better, wiser, stronger.

__________ I have the right to correct my course.

__________ This mistake is a way to look at what I'm doing and see what I want to correct.

__________ This is not really a failure, but efforts toward success. (Babe Ruth)

__________ Instead of "failure," think: Bad choice, bad judgment, missteps, false start, momentary loss of my way, blip, or falling short.

__________ I'm adequate to learn from this and improve next time.

__________ Mistakes show me what I want to improve/correct/what's not working.

__________ I'll be wiser next time.

__________ Mistakes make me human and fallible, just like everyone else.

__________ Okay, I botched that; if at first you don't succeed . . .

__________ Okay, so I mess up 10 percent of the time. The rest of the time I do pretty well.

__________ There's a bright side to this even if I don't see it yet.

__________ Isn't it great that I can do such a ridiculous thing, and still have hope?

__________ Isn't it interesting that I sometimes condemn myself overall for a weakness or imperfection?

__________ I made a mistake. I am not a mistake.

__________ I am more than my mistake. There is more to my life history than this.

__________ I erred; now I'm returning to my good patterns right away.

__________ I did it before. I'll do it again.

__________ I believe things will improve.

__________ Okay, I handled this. I can handle other challenges, too.

__________ This is not the end of the world.

__________ My downfall isn't the end of me.

__________ The sun will come up tomorrow.

__________ No use crying over spilled milk; it's water under the bridge.

__________ No one is a "failure" until he gives up altogether.

__________ I'll not be defeated twice: once by circumstances and once by myself. (Lowell Bennion)

__________ Eventually I'll improve. There will be another chance.

__________ This was a difficult and complex task. It was made more difficult by ______________ (my inexperience, lack of guidance or help, noise, weather, temperature, interruptions, my not feeling up to it, or any other accurate factor).

__________ What will I learn for the next time?

__________ I can't possibly control everything.

__________ Failure is an event, never a person. (Dr. William D. Brown)

__________ Oh, boy! Now I'm really going to learn something. (Harold "Doc" Edgerton)

__________ Failure isn't final. Start again.

__________ Years from now, will anyone really care about this?

## Step Two

Below, write fifteen statements you would most like to remember to tell yourself before, during, and after times when your behavior falls short of your goals (five for before; five for during; and five for after). Statements need not come from the above list.

**"Before" Statements**

1.

2.

3.

4.

5.

**"During" Statements**

1.

2.

3.

4.

5.

**"After" Statements**

1.

2.

3.

4.

5.

During each of the next three days select an event with "flop potential." Spend fifteen minutes mentally rehearsing what you will think before, during, and after the "flop."

For a most amusing and profound treatment of realistic optimism and dealing with failure read Dr. Seuss's *Oh, the Places You'll Go!* (1990).

## Chapter 27

# An Overview of Growing

In this section we have explored important ideas and skills regarding the third building block of self-esteem, Growing. Let's review the key points and skills that you have learned and practiced.

## Active Ideas

- Growing is an ongoing process, never fully completed.
- The growth process is a way of loving. It is satisfying because it starts from the secure inner base of worth and love.
- Emotionally, the process says, "I'm glad inside and unafraid to be Growing—becoming even better."
- Ascent is difficult. Expect hard work.

- Growing is not competitive or comparative. You can select your course and pace. As with weight plans and exercise, it is wise to pick a pace that can be maintained throughout life.
- Growing means elevating others along with self.
- Growing results from applying principles and pleasures that elevate.
- Because Growing is climbing the staircase, not arriving, you need not arrive to experience self-esteem. You need only know in your heart that you're on track and moving ahead.

## Acquired Skills

1. The *Even Though I'm Not Perfect, Nevertheless* ... Skill
2. Just for the Fun of It (Contemplating Possibilities)
3. The Loving, Fearless, Searching, and Honest Moral Inventory
4. Pleasant Activities Scheduling
5. Flop Inoculation

To reinforce these important ideas and skills, please take a few moments to respond to the following questions. You might first wish to flip back through the preceding pages of this section to review what you've done.

1. Which of the ideas have had the most meaning to you?

2. Which skills do you most wish to return to and use again?

3. What do you need right now? Are there skills in this section that you would like to spend more time with? If so, take the time to do so.

Epilogue

# Summing Up

Each person has been created miraculously in so many ways. It is important to quietly recognize and appreciate this so that you may grow with satisfaction and joy.

Don't let mistakes define you. Don't let criticism, falling short of goals, past traumas, lack of money or status, or any other externals define you. Each person is too precious and complex to be so narrowly defined.

In our journey together we have explored a variety of self-esteem building skills. As with any other skills, self-esteem skills take time to acquire and practice to maintain. Perhaps you will incorporate some of these skills into your life without much conscious thought. Perhaps other skills will require that you deliberately set aside some time to practice.

Do not hesitate to go back from time to time to repeat such valuable skills. If life throws you a curve that sets your self-esteem back somewhat, remember to again refer to this book and to rehearse the skills that have had meaning for you. If self-esteem can be built once, it can be built up again.

Like any other important health practice, self-esteem building and maintenance is an ongoing process. However, like other useful habits, self-esteem skills, once acquired, become almost second nature and, therefore, easier to apply.

To summarize and reinforce your most important skills, as well as to serve as a quick reminder during difficult times, please review the entire book, and list below those ideas and skills that you most want to remember.

## Ideas You Want to Remember

## Skills You Want to Remember

# APPENDICES

## Appendix I

# Model for Helping the Person in Distress

The following model depicts how a person experiencing stress can be helped to reduce those symptoms, and the relationship of self-esteem to the restoration of good health.

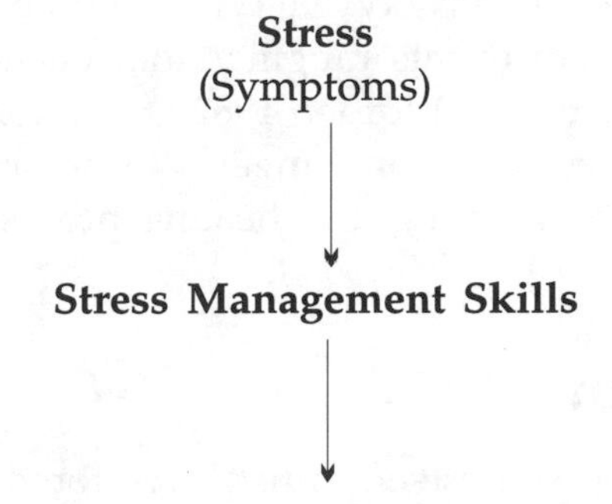

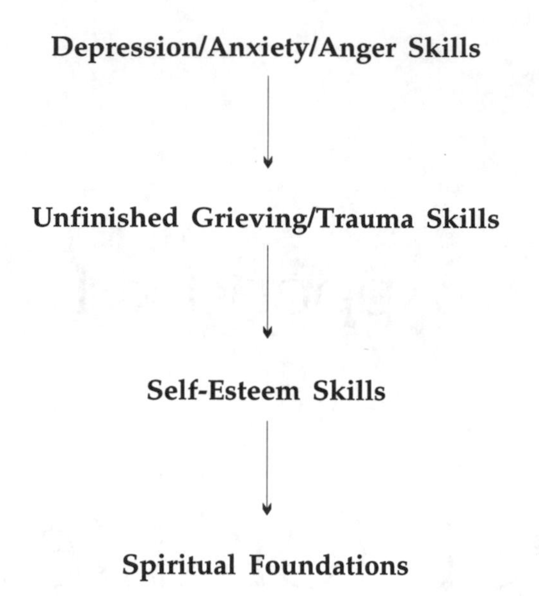


## Managing Stress

"Stress" is a rather general term. The person experiencing stress might manifest symptoms ranging from simple tension, to headaches, fatigue, insomnia, and/or illnesses ranging from high blood pressure to PMS.

Once underlying medical causes are ruled out and/or treated, then stress symptoms can often be reduced by traditional stress management skills, including, for example: systematic relaxation training (progressive muscular relaxation, meditation, autogenics, deep breathing, imagery, etc.), time management, communication skills, exercise and dietary adjustments, yoga, and other coping skills. Such strategies are often quite helpful. If they are not effective, then helpers might look for underlying depression, anxiety, or excessive anger.

For example, clinical depression can often be effectively treated with antidepressant medications, once medical causes have been ruled out. Some people respond very well to cognitive-behavioral skills learned in psychotherapy. Others respond very well to a combination of medication and counseling.

## Unresolved Grief or Trauma

If the above approaches are not completely effective, then helpers might explore unfinished grieving/trauma issues. It is estimated that 15 to 20 percent of people who seek professional counseling for clinical depression or anxiety have at the root of those symptoms unresolved grief/trauma. These can result from events ranging from death of a child or parent, to abuse, amputation, accidents, crime, or job loss (Worden 1982). Symptoms can include emotional numbing, depression, physical stress symptoms, and anger. Worden has identified several active tasks that help the person complete the grieving and healing process and move on.

## Restoring Self-Esteem

It is often observed that damaged self-esteem must be restored before a person will feel whole again. For example, the survivors of sexual abuse usually need to feel a sense of self-worth again before they can release bitterness and the desire for revenge. The person who is chronically angry and defensive will find it easier to withstand criticism once inner security is developed. In some cases, damaged self-esteem can be both a cause and effect of symptoms. For example, low self-esteem can predispose one to depression. Because depression often impairs performance, depression can tend to further lower self-esteem. In either case, developing self-esteem will often help reduce symptoms.

## The Strength of a Spiritual Foundation

Spiritual foundations/skills can help reduce symptoms. For example, one who understands infinite, divine love might find it easier to love and forgive self and others. Respect and regard for all humans might help one understand unconditional human worth. Peace of conscience, forgiveness, and an eternal perspective can help reduce worries.

## Additional Comments

Several points can be noted from this helping model for the person in distress:

1. While a skilled professional can facilitate the reduction of symptoms, the ultimate goal is self-reliance: that the suffering individual will learn the skills that can help prevent the recurrence of symptoms, reduce their severity if they do recur, and/or return the person eventually to optimal health.
2. The helping model is not a rigid model but a flexible one. For example, if it is obvious that a person's symptoms are due to severe clinical depression, then the mental health professional would probably not initially use traditional stress management strategies. Rather, more aggressive approaches to rapidly reduce symptoms would be tried, such as antidepressant medication or electroconvulsive therapy. Cognitive-behavioral psychotherapy and stress management could then be introduced.
3. Self-esteem is sometimes called the common denominator because it underlies so many stress symptoms. Whether low self-esteem is a cause or a result of symptoms, self-esteem skills will often be useful in the reduction of those symptoms. However, this does not eliminate the need for a balanced, comprehensive treatment plan that utilizes all necessary approaches.

# Appendix II

# Forgiving the Self

Almost all cultures have values as to what constitutes right and wrong behavior. In religion, sin refers to behaviors that violate such standards. Guilt is the feeling that alerts one to the wrongness of certain behaviors and motivates one to avoid them. This appendix focuses on healthy guilt, which implies that standards are reasonable, and that the individual assumes appropriate responsibility for one's own behavior, no more no less. The denial of the feeling of healthy guilt has deleterious consequences, just as denial of any feeling does. Shame, as it is often used in contemporary psychology, refers to the unhealthy perception that one is bad to the core.

Repentance implies a return to a former state. Among theologians, there is general agreement as to the steps of repentance, which returns one to a cleansed state characterized by, among other things, God's forgiveness. These steps include:

1. Acknowledge that the behavior was committed and that the behavior was wrong.
2. Acknowledge that hurt was caused to self and others, if others have been hurt by the behavior. It is constructive to feel hurt, sadness, disappointment, and empathy, and to fully realize the connection between these feelings and the behavior that led to them.
3. Confess to God (and others who might have been affected by the behavior) an awareness of the wrong and the consequences of the behavior, and appropriate sorrow for the damage.

4. Make amends when possible (e.g., if something was taken, replace it; or if another's feelings were hurt or self-esteem was damaged, apologize).
5. Forsake the behavior (i.e., determine not to repeat it and take the steps necessary to ensure it does not recur).
6. Commit to holy living. *Holy* derives from the same root as health, and implies wholeness, integration, no divisions between values and behaviors.

After completing the repentance process, some may still find it difficult to forgive the self. So the following ideas might help.

Wrong behaviors are externals. They surround the core, and, like a dirty film, might prevent light from entering or leaving. One might *feel*, therefore, like one is dark and worthless to the core. However, this is a feeling that does not reflect reality. Make sure you interpret the feeling correctly. The sad feeling is a commentary on your behavior that needs to be altered, not your core value! Resist all impulses to interpret the sad feeling as a commentary of worthlessness. When repentance has occurred, one breaks free from the behavior and can more accurately experience core worth again.

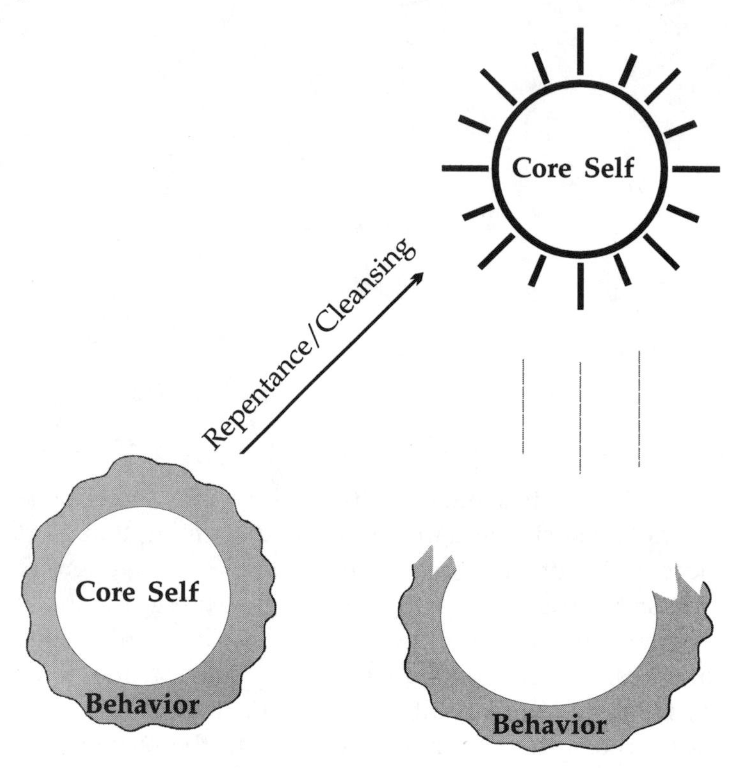


Now the behavior can be remembered but the pain subsides.

As World War II concentration camp survivor Victor Frankl (1978) wrote, "It is a human prerogative to become guilty and it is a human responsibility to overcome guilt." We ask ourselves: How much is left? What can I actively do to embrace responsibility? To improve? To render the past, present, and future meaningful?

# Appendix III

# Touching the Past with Love

Every living soul has experienced painful events in life. Perhaps some of these events still hurt and prevent you from fully experiencing self-esteem. The skill that follows helps one to heal and strengthen emotionally, and to release the painful emotions so that one can move on. The primary agent of healing is love.

This activity is optional because some have a great desire to neutralize the pain of past events and benefit greatly from doing so. Others have no desire to revisit the past. And others would prefer to revisit the past with the help of a mental health professional.

## Directions

1. Find a quiet place where you can be undisturbed for about thirty minutes.
2. Identify an event in your life that is still painful. Such difficult moments might include times when:
   - People hurt/shamed you (e.g., with unkind words, criticism, abuse, bullying, or taunts)

- You felt alone, neglected, rejected, or abandoned
- You were disappointed in your own behavior/performance (e.g., you were overwhelmed and did not know how to cope; your behavior was wrong from an ethical standpoint)

3. Call the person who experienced this difficult time your *younger self.*
4. Call your present self—who possesses greater experience, wisdom, and love—the *wiser self.*
5. Imagine that you, the wiser self, travel back in time to the difficult event, and you approach your younger self. Your younger self looks up and sees you. Your eyes meet and there is an affinity and trust; your younger self is willing to listen to you.
6. You enter into a dialogue with your younger self. You ask the younger self, "What is troubling you?" The younger self expresses the facts *and* feelings of the event. You listen with great empathy and understanding.
7. You ask, "What would help?" You intently listen with your ears and your heart for what is expressed verbally and silently. You perceive and provide for needs, such as the need for:
   - Understanding
   - Instruction. Perhaps you can teach skills that you have recently learned, such as the *Nevertheless* skill
   - Support and Encouragement. (e.g., "Considering your experience and training, you're doing well!"; "It *will* get better!"; "You'll make it through this. I know that you will.")
   - Physical Help or Protection
   - Advice. Think together. Use the experiences and wisdom of both to brainstorm solutions, such as:
     - Perhaps you could advise the child who was abused to say, "That's no way to treat a child." The wiser self stands alongside the child for protection and support.
     - The adult might say to a critical supervisor, "I see your point. I'd like you to help me. I think I'll develop faster if you point out the positives, too."
     - If the younger self behaved in a way that was wrong/unethical, you might explore together the principles and behaviors that favor human growth. Imagine reminding the younger self about these wiser principles and behaviors. Imagine guiding the younger self in applying these behaviors. Then see the younger self actually doing them, and any other helpful behaviors, such as apologizing, expressing sorrow for hurt that the behavior caused, making amends, or expressing kindness. Allow the younger self to experience the more peaceful feelings of the new behaviors, and to share with you what that is like. Provide assurance that this is the wiser course.
   - Above all, communicate love in any or all of the forms that are needed:
     - a loving, gentle, accepting look where eyes meet eyes
     - loving words (e.g., "I love you.")
     - a hug/embrace
     - a soothing touch
8. Tell your younger self that you are returning "back to the future," and that your love will remain with the younger self.

9. Let your attention return to the present. Use a *Nevertheless*-like statement, such as: "That *was* a difficult time, and I love me." Allow the healing feeling of love to sink in and surround you.

Repeat this exercise for a total of four days, using a different difficult event for each day. To reinforce this exercise, it is recommended that you record each experience in writing. Writing it down helps to put the past in perspective and provide distance. It also seems to sharpen and reinforce the solutions.

You might notice somewhat of a drop in mood during the days that you practice this exercise. Thereafter, the mood typically rises above the point at which you began this exercise. This might be likened to lancing a boil—some pain is experienced in order to facilitate healing.

Here is an example of one student's experience with this exercise. This student remembered that when she was a child her mother typically spoke very critically about her father to her. One day the student, as a young child, said something critical about her father in a department store, and her mother shook her violently and screamed, "Don't talk about your father that way." As an adult, the student still remembered how shocked and hurt she felt, and selected this event to work with.

In imagery, the wiser self coached the child to say to her mother, "Why is it that you yelled at me when I said what you wanted and had taught me to say?" The wiser self protected the child but then noticed the pain in the mother's eyes. So she hugged the mother. Then the wiser self told the child that she would miss out if she came back to the present with her. She gave the child a stone as a symbol of comfort and of the love that the wiser self felt for her.

## The Insights of Imagery

Imagery can yield some surprising insights and solutions to difficult past moments. The above is an excellent example of reworking a past event and then concluding by surrounding the pain with love.

If you chose to participate in this four-day exercise, then please complete the following at the end of the four days:

1. Spend one day reviewing the principles and skills that you have learned thus far.

2. Spend three days applying the skills that you found most meaningful.

These steps help to lift the mood again and return the focus to the present.

# Recommended Readings


Bloom, L., K. Coburn, and J. Pearlman. 1975. *The New Assertive Woman*. New York: Delacorte. *Helps people communicate in ways that respect self and others. The book is equally useful for men and women.*

Burns, D. 1980. *Feeling Good*. New York: Signet. *A most practical book on replacing the thinking distortions that cause depression and undermine self-esteem. A very useful application of Aaron Beck's theories.*

Bradshaw, J. 1988. *Healing the Shame That Binds You*. Deerfield Beach, FL: Health Communications. *When shame from neglect, abuse, or criticism has damaged self-esteem and the emotions.*

Seuss, Dr. 1990. *Oh, the Places You'll Go*. New York: Random House. *A clever, humorous treatise on human growth and fallibility. Written for children. Or is it?*

Johnson, H. 1986. *How Do I Love Me?* Salem, WI: Sheffield Publishing Co. *A practical, well-written book on improving self-esteem.*

Kipfer, B. 1990. *14,000 Things To Be Happy About*. New York: Workman. *If part of growing is learning to appreciate the things around us, then this book is part of growing.*

Schiraldi, G. 1996. *Facts to Relax By: A Guide to Relaxation and Stress Reduction.* Send $5.95 to: Utah Valley Regional Medical Center, Education Department, 1134 North 500 West, Suite 204, Provo, UT 84604 (Tel: 801-357-7176). *Detailed instructions for managing stress include: systematic relaxation, exercise, and nutrition guidelines; assertiveness and time management training, changing stressful attitudes; and more.*

Schiraldi, G. 1999. *The Post-Traumatic Stress Disorder Source Book: A Guide to Healing, Recovery, and Growth.* Los Angeles: Lowell House. *When traumatic events, such as abuse, rape, or domestic violence have damaged self-esteem.*

## Scholarly Works

People interested in early scholarly works about the causes and consequences of various levels of self-esteem may refer to:

Coopersmith, S. 1967. *The Antecedents of Self-Esteem*. San Francisco: Freeman.

Rosenberg, M. 1965. *Society and the Adolescent Self-Image*. Princeton, NJ: Princeton University Press.

# Bibliography


Alexander, F. G. 1932. *The Medical Value of Psychoanalysis*. New York: Norton.

Borkovec, T. D., L. Wilkinson, R. Folensbee, et al. 1983. "Stimulus Control Applications to the Treatment of Worry." *Behavior Research and Therapy* 21.

Bourne, R. A., Jr. 1992. *Rational Responses to Four of Ellis' Irrational Beliefs*. Palm Beach Gardens, Fla: The Upledger Institute. (Unpublished class handout.)

Bradshaw, J. 1988. *Healing the Shame That Binds You*. Deerfield Beach, FL.: Health Communications, Inc.

Briggs, D. C. 1977. *Celebrate Yourself: Making Life Work for You*. Garden City, NY: Doubleday.

Brothers, J. 1990. "What Really Makes Men and Women Attractive." *Parade,* August 5.

Brown, S. L., and G. R. Schiraldi. 2000. "Reducing Symptoms of Anxiety and Depression: Combined Results of a Cognitive-Behavioral College Course." Paper presented at Anxiety Disorders Association of America National Conference, Washington, DC, March 24.

Burns, D. 1980. "The Perfectionist's Script for Self-Defeat." *Psychology Today*, November.

Burns, G. 1984. *Dr. Burns' Prescription for Happiness.* New York: G. P. Putnam's Sons.

Canfield, J. 1985. "Body Appreciation" in *Wisdom, Purpose, and Love.* Santa Barbara, CA.: Self-Esteem Seminars/Chicken Soup for the Soul Enterprises. Audiocassette.

———. 1988. "Developing High Self-Esteem in Yourself and Others." Association for Humanistic Psychology, 26th Annual Meeting, Washington, DC, July.

Coopersmith, S. 1967. *The Antecedents of Self-Esteem.* San Francisco: Freeman.

Cousins, N. 1983. *The Healing Heart.* New York: Avon.

De Mello, A. 1990. *Taking Flight: A Book of Story Meditations.* New York: Image Books.

Diener, E. 1984. "Subjective Well-being." *Psychological Bulletin* 95(3):542–575.

Durrant, G. D. 1980. *Someone Special Starring Everyone.* Salt Lake City, UT: Bookcraft Recordings. Audiocassettes

Frankl, V. 1978. *The Unheard Cry for Meaning.* New York: Simon & Schuster.

Gallup Organization. 1992. *Newsweek,* February 17.

Gallwey, W. T. 1974. *The Inner Game of Tennis.* New York: Random House.

Gauthier, J., D. Pellerin, and P. Renaud. 1983. "The Enhancement of Self-Esteem: A Comparison of Two Cognitive Strategies." *Cognitive Therapy and Research* 7(5):389-398.

Greene, B. 1990. Love Finds a Way. *Chicago Tribune,* March 11.

Hafen, B. 1989. *The Broken Heart.* Salt Lake City, UT: Deseret.

Howard, C. A. 1992. Individual Potential Seminars, West, TX. August.

Hunt, D. S., ed. 1987. *Love: A Fruit Always in Season.* Bedford, NH: Ignatius Press.

Kipfer, B. A. 1990. *14,000 Things to Be Happy About.* New York: Workman Publishing

Lazarus, A. A. 1984. "Multimodal Therapy" in *Current Psychotherapies,* 3d ed., edited by R. J. Corsini. Itasca, IL: Peacock.

Leman, K., and R. Carlson. 1989. *Unlocking the Secrets of Your Childhood Memories.* Nashville: Thomas Nelson.

Levin, P. 1988. *Cycles of Power.* Deerfield Beach, FL: Health Communications, Inc.

Lewinsohn, P. M., R. F. Munoz, M. A. Youngren, and A. M. Zeiss. 1986. *Control Your Depression.* New York: Prentice Hall.

Linville, P. W. 1987. "Self-Complexity as a Cognitive Buffer Against Stress-Related Illness and Depression." *Journal of Personality & Social Psychology* 52(4):663-676.

Lowry, R. J., ed. 1973. *Dominance, Self-Esteem, Self-Actualization: Germinal Papers of A. H. Maslow.* Monterey, CA: Brooks/Cole.

Maslow, A. 1968. *Toward a Psychology of Being,* 2d ed. New York: Van Nostrand Reinhold.

Maxwell, N. A. 1976. "Notwithstanding My Weakness." *Ensign,* November.

Mecca, A., N. Smelser, and J. Vasconcellos. 1989. *The Social Importance of Self-Esteem.* Berkeley, CA: University of California Press.

Meichenbaum, D. 1985. *Stress Inoculation Training.* New York: Pergamon.

Michelotti, J. 1991. "My Most Unforgettable Character." *Reader's Digest,* April.

Mills Brothers. 1983. "You're Nobody Till Somebody Loves You." CBS Records/CBS Inc.

Montegu, A. 1988. "Growing Young: The Functions of Laughter and Play." Power of Laughter and Play Conference. Toronto, Canada.

Morgan, W. P. 1984. *Coping with Mental Stress: The Potential & Limits of Exercise Intervention* (Final Report). Bethesda, NIMH, pp. 11–14. Cited in W. P. Morgan. 1985. "Affective Beneficence of Vigorous Physical Activity." *Medicine & Science in Sports & Exercise* 17(1):94-100.

National Geographic Society. 1986. *The Incredible Machine.* Washington, DC.

Nelson, R. M. 1988. *The Power Within Us,* Salt Lake City, UT: Deseret.

Nouwen, H. J. M. 1989. *Lifesigns : Intimacy, Fecundity and Ecstasy in Christian Perspective.* New York: Image Books.

Patinkin, M. 1991. "Little Things That Make Life Worth Living." *Providence Journal-Bulletin,* April 24

Pennebaker, J. W. 1997. *Opening Up: The Healing Power of Expressing Emotion*. New York: Guilford.

Peterson, C., M. Seligman, and G. Vaillant. 1988. "Pessimistic Explanatory Style as a Risk Factor for Physical Illness: A Thirty-Five-Year Longitudinal Study." *Journal of Personality and Social Psychology*. (55):23–27

Petrie, A., and J. Petrie. 1986. *Mother Teresa.* San Francisco, CA: Dorason Corporation. Videocassette.

Piburn, S., ed. 1993. *The Dalai Lama a Policy of Kindness : An Anthology of Writings by and about the Dalai Lama/Winner of the Nobel Peace Prize*. Ithaca, NY: Snow Lion Publications.

Pippert, R. M. 1999. *Out of the Salt Shaker and into the World: Evangelism as a Way of Life*. Downers Grove, IL: Intervarsity Press.

Ratcliff, J. D. 1967–1974. "I Am Joe's . . ." series. *Reader's Digest*.

Richards, S. L. 1955. *Where is Wisdom? Addresses of President Stephen L. Richards*. Salt Lake City, UT: Deseret Book.

Rogers, F. M. 1970. *It's You I Like.* Pittsburgh, PA: Fred M. Rogers and Family Communications, Inc.

Rorty, R. 1991. "Heidegger, Kundera and Dickens," in *Essays on Heidegger and Others.* New York: Cambridge University Press.

Schiraldi, G. R., and S. L. Brown. 2001. "Primary Prevention for Mental Health: Results of an Exploratory Cognitive-Behavioral College Course." *The Journal for Primary Prevention*: 22(1).

Schlossberg, L., and G. D. Zuidema. 1997. *The Johns Hopkins Atlas of Human Functional Anatomy* 4th ed. Baltimore: Johns Hopkins University Press.

Schor, J. 1991. "Workers of the World, Unwind." *Technology Review,* November/December.

Seuss, Dr. 1990. *Oh, the Places You'll Go*. New York: Random House.

Sharapan, H. 1992. Associate Producer, Family Communications, Inc.: Pittsburgh, PA. Personal communication, August 20.

Sonstroem, R. J. 1984. Exercise and Self-Esteem. In *Exercise and Sports Sciences Reviews*, vol. 12. R. L. Terjung, ed. Lexington, MA: The Collamore Press, pp. 123-155.

Tamarin, A., ed. 1969. *Benjamin Franklin: An Autobiographical Portrait*. London: MacMillan.

Thayer, R. E. 1989. *The Biopsychology of Mood and Arousal*. New York: Oxford University Press.

Worden, J. W. 1982. *Grief Counseling and Grief Therapy: A Handbook for the Mental Health Practitioner*. New York: Springer.

**Glenn R. Schiraldi**, Ph.D., has served on the stress management faculties at the Pentagon and the University of Maryland, where he received the Outstanding Teaching Award in the College of Health and Human Performance. He is the author of various articles and books on human mental and physical health, including *The Post-Traumatic Stress Disorder Source Book: A Guide to Healing, Recovery, and Growth; Conquer Anxiety, Worry, and Nervous Fatigue: A Guide to Greater Peace; Hope and Help for Depression: A Practical Guide; Facts to Relax By: A Guide to Relaxation and Stress Reduction; Stress Management Strategies*, and *The Anger Management Source Book: Paths to a Calmer, More Peaceful Existence*. Glenn's writing excellence has been recognized by various scholarly and popular sources, including the *Washington Post, American Journal of Health Promotion, the Mind/Body Health Review*, and *the International Stress and Tension Control Society Newsletter*.

Serving at the University of Maryland since 1980, he has pioneered a number of mind/body courses, teaching coping skills to adults across a wide range of ages. His *Stress and the Healthy Mind* course, upon which this book is based, raised self-esteem, while lowering symptoms of depression, anxiety, and hostility. His research interests at the university center on personality and stress, including self-esteem, depression, anxiety, resilience, and post-traumatic stress. At the Pentagon, he helped to design and implement a series of prototype courses in stress management for the Department of the Army—including hostility/anger management, systematic relaxation, and communication skills.

He serves on the Board of Directors of the Depression and Related Affective Disorders Association, a Johns Hopkins University Department of Psychiatry cooperative, and the editorial board of the *International Journal of Emergency Mental Health*. A graduate of the U.S. Military Academy, West Point, he holds graduate degrees from Brigham Young University and the University of Maryland.